Did the Old Testament Endorse Slavery?

# Did the Old Testament Endorse Slavery?

Joshua Bowen

---

**Digital Hammurabi Press**

**Mechanicsville, MD.**

# Contents

# Preface

In the two years that I have been engaging with people on social media, I have seen few topics come up in conversation as much as *biblical slavery*. Those who are antagonistic toward the Christian religion are quick to cite the topic, particularly as it appears in the Old Testament... and rightfully so. The fact is, laws concerning the appropriate practice of slavery are not only present in the Hebrew Bible, but they can also be quite shocking. Fathers can sell their daughters into slavery. Foreign slaves can be kept for life and passed on as inherited property. Slaves can – are even expected to – be beaten with a wooden rod. Indeed, to our modern sense of morality, such practices are to be condemned.

How should we approach such a hot-button issue? Most of the arguments that I have seen on social media – particularly those in video or blog format – tackle the relevant passages and concepts from either an anti- or pro-Christian perspective. Unfortunately, while each side of the debate has good points to make, the discussion is often left at an unmovable standoff, with either side vehemently opposed to genuinely understanding the point of view of the other.

This book is an attempt to bridge that gulf. There are two pieces of the puzzle that are missing from the discussions/debates described above. First, as noted, is the frequent lack of desire to truly understand the position of those holding an opposing viewpoint. This book is designed to address aspects of *both* sides of the topic of slavery in the Old Testament, including points of evidence that appear to support both the pro- and anti-Christian positions.

Second, there is a gross misunderstanding – in my opinion – of the broader context in which the Hebrew Bible was written. Specifically, there are ideas floating about concerning what other ancient Near Eastern cultures were like, and how the Old Testament greatly improved upon practices such as slavery. Our goal here is to paint a picture of slavery in the Hebrew Bible that can be situated within its well-defined ANE context.

By seriously considering and addressing the data that is cited on both sides of this issue, and by illuminating the ancient contexts in which these OT laws were written, it is my hope that the reader will find in these pages information pertinent to placing Old Testament slavery in its proper historical and literary context.

# Thanks and Acknowledgements

I would like to thank my wife, Megan, for enduring the many hours of required research and writing that went into this publication, along with the innumerable conversations on the not-so-joyful subject of slavery. She is also singularly responsible for the editing and publication of the book, and her patience with me in matters of formatting is also to be praised.

I would also like to thank Skylar Fiction for his enthusiasm in partnering with me in debates and discussions on social media on the topic of slavery in the Old Testament. While it is an interesting and thought-provoking subject, one might argue that it approached repetition *ad nauseum*, and his willingness to continue discussing the topic positively influenced the formulation of the book as you now have it.

Finally, I would like to thank the supporters and fans of our YouTube channel, Digital Hammurabi. The unwavering stream of positive reinforcement has made this process far more enjoyable.

# INTRODUCTION

Abraham Lincoln once wrote, "If slavery is not wrong, nothing is wrong."[1] It is clear, particularly in light of relatively recent history here in the United States, that owning another human being is immoral by modern standards. To the surprise of many, however, the abhorrent practice of slavery appears prominently in the Old Testament (also called the Hebrew Bible). As it occurs with some frequency in the Old Testament, the issue of slavery often surfaces as a source of contention in discussions about morality, specifically concerning its implications for God's own character: how could a loving God have endorsed slavery? As my grandfather often says, it is a topic that usually generates more heat than light.

There is little doubt that the laws of the Old Testament identified and discussed the proper practice of slavery. The debate today often focuses on whether or not the Old Testament laws condoned or even endorsed it. If slavery was

---

[1] Letter from Abraham Lincoln to Albert G. Hodges, April 4, 1864 (www.loc.gov/resources, cited July 19, 2019).

endorsed, which type of slavery was being described? Was it indentured servitude or debt-slavery (which many would compare to a type of voluntary employment or general debt repayment, like working at McDonalds or owning a credit card), or were there actually chattel-slaves who were owned and passed down to the children of the owners as inheritance? The answers to these, and other slavery-related questions, are not only important for understanding the ancient Near Eastern context of Iron Age Israelite culture, but they also inform and shape interpretations of the Old Testament and Christian theology.

There is an odd dichotomy that appears in this discussion, which leads to a great deal of unnecessary confusion. On the one hand, we can read about what experts in the fields of biblical and ancient Near Eastern studies say about topics like slavery in the Old Testament. On the other hand, we can see what is *actually debated* on social media, (e.g., YouTube, Twitter, and Facebook). In my experience, much (if not most) of the scholarly research that has been done on this topic – and others like it – does not make its way out of the proverbial ivory tower into the public arena.

This disconnect between what scholars have discovered and what non-specialists are aware of was the primary motivation for the creation of our YouTube channel, *Digital Hammurabi*. Having spent years in graduate school – enduring the rigors of our doctoral programs – we were absolutely shocked by the lack of reputable scholarly information that appears in so many online debates and discussions. In an attempt to bridge the gap between scholars and non-specialists, we provide a resource for normal, everyday people to access and understand the research that has already gone into so many of these hotly debated topics. It is with this in mind that I write this book.

I hope to accomplish three primary goals with this publication. First and foremost, I want to make available to the reader the vast amount of reputable, peer-reviewed, scholarly research that has already gone into the topic of slavery in the Hebrew Bible and the wider ancient Near East. It is not my intent to provide new, groundbreaking discoveries or radical conclusions concerning this issue. Instead, I wish to demonstrate that there is general consensus among scholars when it comes to the nature and reality of many aspects of slavery in the ancient world. Thus, you will see me reference a myriad of scholars, including

Introduction

many "liberal" and "conservative" authors, quoting them
frequently in the body of the text, as presenting their
research is directly related to my primary goal.[2]

Second, I want to present this scholarly consensus in a clear
and palatable fashion. One of the criticisms often leveled
against the academic community is the lack of relatability
that their writing has when it comes to the general public. It
is difficult, of course, to engage in detailed and exhaustive
research to solve difficult problems or elucidate new
information on a narrow topic, while simultaneously making
that information relatable and relevant to people who are not
specialists in the field. It is my hope that this book will act as
a link between these two groups, taking the detailed and
nuanced conclusions of scholars and packaging them in a
way that everyone can understand.

My third and final goal will be to provide some practical
application for all of this information on ancient slavery. As I
have stated, Old Testament slavery is constantly debated;
those who believe the Bible to be the inspired Word of God

---

[2] On the use of the terms "liberal" and "conservative" in this context, see
Grabbe 1987.

4

tend to defend Old Testament slavery, attempting to explain difficult passages in a way that makes the practice seem less immoral by today's standards. On the opposite side, atheists and agnostics tend to seek out and highlight the most detestable aspects of the practice in order to demonize the god of the Old Testament. However, as neither side generally has ready access to scholarly research on the topic, some of their conclusions end up being too extreme. It is my hope that, by clearly articulating what slavery was actually like in the Old Testament and in the ancient Near East, both sides of this discussion will be armed with reputable data, and will be able to move the conversation forward in a more meaningful and productive way.

I want to take a moment and talk about what I mean when I mention "scholarly consensus," particularly as it relates to Old Testament and ancient Near Eastern slavery. When we talk about scholarly consensus, we are generally referring to what mainstream scholars in a particular field agree to be the case concerning a particular topic. There are obviously many issues on which scholars do not completely agree, usually in what we would consider the specific details of the subject. However, in this book, we are concerned with things that scholars generally *do* agree on concerning Old

## Introduction

Testament and ancient Near Eastern slavery. How and why do scholars come to general agreement on these issues? Do they all have a big meeting where they take a vote: "All in favor of the Hebrew Bible endorsing slavery raise your hand"? No, of course not. Neither is there some grand conspiracy involving "liberal" scholars, laughing menacingly as they plot the destruction of organized religion in the world.

The reality is that there are certain facts or "data points" that each scholar or researcher uses when attempting to make sense of an issue. If you have ever seen a murder mystery, the detective in the story is armed with certain facts or details about the case. Some of these might include: 1) the accused was found with a revolver in his hand; 2) the revolver had been recently fired; 3) the murder victim was killed by a bullet from that same revolver. These three data points (the recently fired weapon in the accused's hand and the death by the fired bullet) are some of the facts with which the detective must develop a reconstruction of what happened. The more evidence or facts that the detective can uncover, the more detail he will have, and the higher the likelihood that he will be able to create a scenario or interpretation of the facts that accords well with what actually happened.

The same is true when we study the ancient world. For example, let's say that an archaeologist excavates a site, uncovers the buildings, vessels, and remains of the people who lived at that site, and from these data points, develops an interpretation that best explains the evidence or data that they have uncovered. However, the archaeologist also discovers clay tablets that contain writing. Not only are the physical tablets themselves part of their data set, but also the writing that the tablets contain. A linguist will decipher the writing and determine things like what the tablet says, who wrote it, the genre of the text, and so on. This information is then added to the growing data set that scholars use to "paint a picture," not only of that particular excavated site, but of the geographical region, the entire period, or even aspects of the ancient world as a whole.

Thus, when we consider a topic like slavery in the Hebrew Bible or in the ancient Near East, a good researcher will seek to identify as much information as possible concerning the topic. What evidence from legal "codes" do we have? What about actual legal texts, like court cases? Are there any cases in existence that we have discovered? What about stories from the period? Do they speak of slavery? If so, what do they say? When all of the available data have been gathered, the scholar attempts to piece it all together, creating an interpretive model that best explains all of the available evidence or data points.

Forming an interpretation that best accounts for all of the data is absolutely critical. If the detective from our example above were to conclude, "I think that the victim died from a stab wound," the evidence of the gunshot wound would appear not to be accounted for in his interpretation. Thus, he would either have to account for or explain why it appears that the victim died from a gunshot, but was actually killed by a stab wound. In the same way, if someone concluded that Hebrew slaves were allowed to be kept for life against their will in the laws of the Hebrew Bible, they would likely not be taking into account the evidence from passages like Exodus 21 which appears to contradict that conclusion. They would have to explain how the data from Exodus 21 fits into their interpretive model.

This brings us back to scholarly consensus. Why is it that, on the whole, scholars appear to agree about a great many aspects of slavery in the Old Testament and ancient Near East? It is because they are ostensibly dealing with the same data points. For example, they have all read Exodus 21, Deuteronomy 15, 20, and Leviticus 25. They all know about Nehemiah 5 and Jeremiah 34. Thus, they must formulate an interpretation that accounts for the data in all of these passages (as well as many more pieces of evidence). Thus, there will be broad agreement on the basic "facts of the case." Where we frequently find disagreement, however, is in the interpretation of certain details of slavery. "Who is this particular verse about: a debt-slave or a chattel-slave?" "What does 'punish' mean in Exodus 21:20: to *kill* the master, or to *punish* him as the judges see fit?" "Does Exodus 21:16 refer to kidnapping Israelite citizens, or everyone in general?" In short, you will find as you read this book that there is general scholarly consensus on many or most aspects of slavery in the Old Testament and ancient Near East, and this is the result of reputable scholars having access to the same data points and attempting to make sense of them within their interpretative models.

The book will be structured in the following way. I will begin by providing a general overview and description of slavery in the Old Testament. What types of slavery existed? How did

9

one become a slave? Did slaves have any rights? Were they considered property? The goal of the first chapter will not necessarily be to provide detailed evidence or support for the characteristics presented; this will come later in the book. The goal in chapter one will simply be to provide a clear summary of what slavery in the Hebrew Bible looked like.

In chapter two, we will widen our scope to the ancient Near East, not only from the period of the biblical texts, but from the periods leading up to it. We will examine the so-called "law codes," including the famous Code of Hammurabi, to see what they say about slavery. Because we have a great deal of documentation that has survived from the ancient Near East, we will also examine other legal texts, as well as other textual genres, in order to glean information useful to the discussion. Of course, it will not be possible to examine all or even most of the available evidence. However, I will attempt to deal with the relevant data points as much as possible.

Chapter three will focus on a more detailed analysis of the primary legal passages that deal with slavery: Exodus 21, Deuteronomy 15, 20, and Leviticus 25. As there was very likely development between the earlier book of Exodus and the later books of Deuteronomy and Leviticus, we will examine how the laws concerning slavery may have changed, and who benefited from these developments. We will also examine in greater detail issues like slaves as war plunder, rules for the release of slaves, the meaning of "property," etc.

Finally, in chapter four, we will turn our attention to some of the more common objections that I have received when discussing the issues surrounding slavery in the ancient world that are not covered in the first three chapters. "Does 'forever' in Leviticus 25:44-46 actually mean 'for all time?'" "Doesn't Deuteronomy 23:15-16 demonstrate that slaves can run away if they so choose, and the Israelites are commanded *not* to return them? Doesn't this do away with the idea of slavery?" "Leviticus 19 tells Israel to love foreigners. You can't have slavery *and* have a command to love foreigners. These things are mutually exclusive." I will seek to answer these (and other) questions and objections, hopefully providing clarity and solutions that are reasonable and supported by the data.

In the end, it is my hope that the reader will be armed with a great deal of reputable scholarly research concerning slavery, not only in the Hebrew Bible, but also in the wider ancient Near East. They will be able to answer such questions as,

Introduction

"What was Old Testament slavery like?" "What were the different forms of slavery?" "Was slavery in the Hebrew Bible essentially different from slavery in the ancient Near East?" and "Would slavery in the Old Testament be considered immoral today?" By obtaining such clarification and precision on this topic, which is so hotly debated in the public arena, we will hopefully be able to move the conversation forward, not only to understand slavery in the ancient world, but also to better understand and orient oneself to Christian religion and theology.

# CHAPTER ONE:

# Slavery in the Old Testament: An Overview

*Slavery is a condition acknowledged in the Pentateuch in which a person is deprived of freedom, at least for a period of time, by being in subjugation to a master in order that the master may benefit from the labor of the slave. Slavery may be involuntary, in which case the slave is generally considered the property of the owner and, as such, may be bought and sold. In Pentateuchal legislation, involuntary permanent slavery applies only to non-Israelites. Slavery may also be voluntary for Israelites, such as when they agree to work for fellow Israelites for a limited period of time to pay off debts or to survive poverty or destitution. But, because God brought the Israelites out of slavery in Egypt to serve him alone as master, they are forbidden to bring fellow Israelites into a condition of permanent*

*slavery, as was the case in the rest of the*
*ancient Near East. Permanent slavery is*
*permitted only for a Gentile in subjection to a*
*Hebrew. The Israelites' identity as people*
*redeemed from slavery has direct implications*
*for the forms of slavery that existed in Israel*
*and their treatment of their slaves, both Gentile*
*chattel slaves and Hebrew bondservants.*[3]

In most of my discussions on social media concerning slavery in the Old Testament, I have found that people tend to automatically compare Old Testament slavery to the practice of slavery before the Civil War, or Antebellum slavery. This is often done to draw attention to the horrors of Antebellum slavery, which will then set the standard for the rest of our discussion. This will "muddy the waters" in the discussion, as many people assume that when the word *slavery* is used, it must refer to the same practice that, for example, we see portrayed in movies set in the pre-Civil War era. One of the most important first steps that we can take in developing a clear understanding of slavery in the Old Testament and in

---

[3] Haas 2003: 778.

the ancient Near East is *clearly defining our terms*. What do we mean when we talk about "slavery?"

While the definition of slavery can have nuanced meanings depending on the context in which the term is used, there are essential aspects that can be seen throughout.[4] As Gene Haas defined slavery above, it is a state in which someone is deprived of their freedom, subjected to another individual, who benefits from their labor; this state can exist temporarily or permanently. Dandamayev defines slavery in this way: "Slavery is the institution whereby one person can hold ownership rights over another."[5] Perhaps a good working definition for our purposes might be, "A condition in which an individual is owned by another. The owner controls and benefits from the actions and activities of the owned individual." We will see that there were different types of slavery described in the Hebrew Bible, and we will attempt

---

[4] Culbertson 2011: 7. "It is impossible to cite every occasion at which a scholar lamented the troubles associated with defining slavery." For a lengthy discussion on the difficulties associated with assigning such a universal definition, see pp. 7-11 of Culbertson's article.

[5] Dandamayev 1992: 58.

to further specify this more general definition when discussing these types.

When discussing slavery in ancient Israel, we are more limited in our sources than if we were discussing slavery as was known in the wider ancient Near East. Generally speaking, we are usually restricted to the information that we can gather from the copies of the texts that comprise what we refer to as the Old Testament or the Hebrew Bible. To put this into perspective, when we come to chapter two and examine the evidence for slavery in the ancient Near East, we will see that our sources are often the original legal texts or documents from their actual time of writing. That's right: we actually have the original tablets and stelae on which these texts were written, not simply copies of the originals (or copies of copies). However, with the Hebrew Bible, we are most often left with only copies of the originals, which requires a rather different approach to accessing the data.

The information that we can gather from the Hebrew Bible comes from a variety of textual genres. We obviously rely heavily on the legal passages found in Exodus, Leviticus, and Deuteronomy to inform our understanding of what the laws or legal traditions ostensibly were. We also have references to practices concerning slavery in the various narratives in the Old Testament, but these require a more nuanced approach, as they may not reflect the ideals of the law, but simply their application (or lack thereof). For example, in Nehemiah 5, we see that the Jews were selling other Jews into slavery in a way that was contrary to the law. Thus, this can tell us about how slavery was practiced (at least in this context), but it does not necessarily tell us what the ideal was according to the law. We also see mention of slavery in the prophetic texts, which can illuminate our understanding of the position of the prophets on the practice. Finally, when we view didactic texts, like the proverbs, we can see more common ideas or customs related to slavery.

There have been different kinds of slavery throughout history – some more horrific than others according to our modern standards. However, in the Old Testament, we see essentially two different types of slavery: debt and chattel. Tigay writes:

> "There are two types of servants in biblical law: indentured servants and full slaves. Both are termed *'eved,* 'servant.' Servitude was an accepted fact of life in Israel as it was

everywhere in the ancient world . . .
Furthermore, full lifelong slavery is in
principle limited to foreigners. Israelites may
only become indentured servants and may not
be held indefinitely against their wishes."[6]

Debt-slavery generally consisted of a person pledging their services to another in order to repay a debt. As the owner "controls the actions and activities of the owned individual" in debt-slavery, the master owns the services of the slave, but not their personhood, and only until the debt is repaid. Chattel-slavery, on the other hand, involves the slave being owned as chattel (or moveable property). In this scenario, the slave is owned by the master permanently, and can be passed down as inheritance to his children.

It is important for us to see that there were laws in place to establish the appropriate practice of slavery in the Hebrew Bible. Let's begin with the laws concerning debt-slavery. In the legal texts, debt-slaves are generally associated with the Israelites. This is not to say that foreigners could not become debt-slaves, as they most certainly could. However, the law

---

[6] Tigay 1996: 147-148.

states in both Exodus and Deuteronomy that Israelites could *only* be taken temporarily as debt-slaves. In Exodus 21:2-6, we see a Hebrew male who was sold into debt-slavery. In this situation, the law required that he serve six years, after which he would go out free, without debt. This is also seen in Deuteronomy 15:12-18, although scholars generally agree that this passage shows a development in the law of debt-slavery concerning Israelites. While the slave was still only to serve six years, when he was released, he was to be amply provided for by the master, in order that he might not fall into poverty again. In Leviticus 25, an even later text, we see that the law had been developed even further. For example, in verses 39-43, if a fellow Israelite were to fall into debt-slavery, he was to work until the year of Jubilee (the 50th year), when he would be released. However, he was not to work as a "slave" (עֶבֶד *'eved*), but as a "hired worker." In other words, Leviticus 25 improves on the conditions of debt-slavery one step further. Now, this is not to say that the laws were actually carried out in this way; we see in passages like Nehemiah 5 and Jeremiah 34 that debt-slaves were often not released, or were taken back after release.

The second type of slavery in the Old Testament is chattel-slavery. Generally speaking, we define a slave as chattel if

19

the slave's status is not contingent upon their debt to the master. In his discussion on slavery during the early second millennium B.C.E. in Mesopotamia, Westbrook distinguishes between debt- and chattel-slavery in this way:

> "Debt slaves were free persons who had entered slavery by reason of a debt . . . They were alienable, but their slavery was conditional upon the existence of the debt and would be terminated with its extinction, for whatever reason. Chattel slaves were slaves who had entered slavery on any other basis and whose slavery was in theory permanent and unconditional."[7]

In Leviticus 25:44-46, which stands in direct contrast to the laws concerning Hebrew debt-slaves, we see that foreigners from the surrounding nations, as well as those who are sojourners in the land of Israel, can be purchased as chattel-slaves.

---

[7] Westbrook 2003b: 380.

"Your male and female slaves are to come from
the nations around you; from them you may
buy slaves. You may also buy some of the
temporary residents living among you and
members of their clans born in your country,
and they will become your property. You can
bequeath them to your children as inherited
property and can make them slaves for life,
but you must not rule over your fellow
Israelites ruthlessly"
(Lev. 25:44-46 NIV).[8]

Concerning v. 44, Milgrom notes:

"The assumption here is that the alien is a
chattel-slave, not a debt-slave. This is
confirmed by the verb *qānâ,* 'purchase.' A non-
Israelite chattel-slave is defined as a *miqneh
kesep* 'purchased' (Gen. 17:12-13, 23, 27; Exod.

---

[8] I will use the New International Version (NIV) for biblical quotations.

12:44) or simply as *kaspô* 'his property' (Exod. 21:21)."[9]

Slaves could not only be purchased, but they could also be born into slavery. As we will see in a later chapter, Exodus 21:4 describes children born to a slave who remain the property of the master. Other passages speak of a house-born slave as "one born of the house" (יְלִיד בַּיִת *yelid bayit*). In Leviticus 22:10-11 we read:

> "No one outside a priest's family may eat the sacred offering, nor may the guest of a priest or his hired worker eat it. But if a priest buys a slave with money, or if slaves are born in his household, they may eat his food."

We see slaves born into servitude in Genesis 17:12, as well as Jeremiah 2:4. The author of Ecclesiastes himself boasts of his great wealth, which included slaves: "I bought male and female slaves and had other slaves who were born in my house. I also owned more herds and flocks than anyone in

---

[9] Milgrom 2001: 2230.

Jerusalem before me" (Eccles. 2:7).[10] Mendelsohn summarizes:

> "The Old Testament terminology corresponds to that in Mesopotamia: yelid bayit 'houseborn slave,' in distinction to miqnat kesef 'purchased slave'; ben bayit 'son of the house,' and anše bayit 'people of the household' or 'domestics.' The latter term includes both houseborn and purchased slaves, as is evident from Genesis 17:27: 'And all the people of his house, born in the house and bought with silver.'"[11]

---

[10] See Longman 1997: 91. "Qohelet's large property holdings required many servants, and in this verse he tells us that he owned both male and female servants, whom he purchased, as well as their offspring, born while their parents were working for him; as a result, they also belonged to him. Genesis 15:3 and 17:12, 27 appear aware of such a distinction. Exodus 21:2-11 comments that though a Hebrew slave only must serve for seven years, any children that he has during this time belong to the master."

[11] Mendelsohn 1978: 58.

We see, therefore, that there were basically two types of slaves in the Old Testament: debt- and chattel-slaves. But this raises an obvious question: how did someone become a slave? There were several avenues to slavery. We have already established that a person could enter into debt servitude, and that the service of a Hebrew slave was temporary, while the foreigner could be held permanently. Slaves could also be purchased, whether Hebrew (Exod. 21:2; Deut. 15:12) or foreign (Exod. 12:44; Lev. 22:11; 25:44-46). One could also become a chattel-slave by being born into slavery (Exod. 12:44; 21:4), captured in war (Deut. 20:10-15), or as the result of judicial punishment (Exod. 22:2).

Propp summarizes:

> "Persons mostly entered servitude due to
> economic distress (Lev. 25:39; Deut. 15:12;
> 28:68; Isa. 50:1; Amos 2:6; 8:6). Throughout the
> Near East, debt was the main cause of slavery
> (Mendelson 1949; 1955: 66; Chirichigno 1993).
> Other ways to become a slave were sale by
> parents (Exod. 21:7; 2 Kgs. 4:1; Neh. 5:2, 5),
> also due to poverty; judicial sentence (Exod.
> 22:2); kidnapping (Gen. 37:28; Exod. 21:16;

Deut. 24:7), and capture in war (Gen. 14:12-14; Num. 31:9, 18; Deut. 21:10-14; 1 Sam. 30:3; 1 Kgs. 20[¹]:39; 2 Kgs. 5:2; 2 Chr. 28:8-15). There was also the yelid bayit 'house-born,' the offspring of slaves (see Gen. 14:14; 17:12, 23, 27; Exod. 21:4-5; Lev. 22:11; 25:45-46; Jer. 2:14). After becoming a slave, during the term of servitude one was a chattel, much like domestic cattle (Gen. 12:16; 20:14; 24:35; 30:43), i.e., owned but still possessed of some basic rights and the object of empathy (cf. Job 31:13-15)."[12]

One of the challenging aspects of the slavery laws in the Hebrew Bible is distinguishing between regulations for owning *debt-slaves* and those for owning *chattel-slaves*. Chirichigno writes:

"While various laws show a special concern for the well-being of a slave, there is nevertheless some confusion as to whom these slave laws apply, since the term עבד 'slave', and similar

---

[12] Propp 2006: 188.

terms, are employed in most of the slave laws
of the Old Testament. That is, do these slave
laws apply exclusively to foreign chattel-
slaves, or to Israelite debt-slaves, or to both
types of slaves?"[13]

There is a great deal of debate concerning this issue,
particularly with respect to Exodus 21. In a later section,
when we analyze Exodus 21, we will see some of the reasons
why these ambiguous passages are debated.

Was slavery voluntary or involuntary? Strictly speaking,
much of the slavery that we see in the Old Testament was
voluntary: that is, one could sell himself, or those under his
control, into slavery in order to stave off poverty or to make
good on a debt. However, two things need to be understood.
First, involuntary slavery clearly existed in the Hebrew Bible
(e.g., slavery by birth, women and children enslaved as
plunder during wartime, etc.). Second, although other types
of slavery were technically or legally voluntary, passages like
2 Kings 4 and Jeremiah 34 tell us that one could be taken
into slavery against their will in the moment, and that, once

---

[13] Chirichigno 1993: 146-147.

enslaved (even as a debt-slave), one was under the control of the master, and could be kept against one's will. Thus, concerning the shared legal tradition of the Old Testament and ancient Near East, Westbrook summarizes, "Although, in practice, economic circumstances would often force a person into slavery, in law his act was voluntary."[14] In other words, we must be very careful when we seek to identify whether an individual entered into slavery of his own volition; there is often a distinction between *practical* volition and *legal* volition.

To further define what slavery looked like in the Old Testament, we will now move into some of the laws concerning the treatment of slaves. As mentioned above, it is difficult at times for scholars to determine whether a particular law deals with a debt-slave, a chattel-slave, or both. Some general statements can be made, however. For example, slaves were expected to be physically punished. In Proverbs 29:19-21 we read:

> "Servants cannot be corrected by mere words;
> though they understand, they will not respond.

---

[14] Westbrook 2009b: 215.

Do you see someone who speaks in haste?
There is more hope for a fool than for them. A
servant pampered from youth will turn out to
be insolent."

In his commentary on Proverbs 10-31, Michael Fox notes
concerning this passage:

> "The proverb gives advice for managing a
> household. Since a slave is deprived of
> material interests of his own, he must, it was
> presumed, be beaten into submission, like a
> brute animal or a fool. Slaves were apparently
> felt to be of a qualitatively lower order . . .
> Strict treatment of slaves is advised again in
> 29:21."[15]

While this might sound unnecessarily violent, it is the same
discipline that we see expected for children. "Whoever spares
the rod hates their children, but the one who loves their
children is careful to discipline them" (Prov. 13:24), and "Do

---

[15] Fox 2009: 843.

not withhold discipline from a child; if you punish them with the rod, they will not die" (Prov. 23:13).

This type of discipline can also be seen in Exodus 21:20-21, where a master strikes his male or female slave with a "rod" (שֵׁבֶט *shevet*), the same Hebrew word that was used in some of the passages above. If the slave were to die as a direct result of the beating, then it would be assumed that the master was intending to kill them (or at least do more than discipline). If the slave survived a day or two following the beating, then it would be assumed that the master did not intend to do more than discipline the slave, and would thus receive no punishment, as the slave was "his money." A few verses later (vv. 26-27), we see that if the master were to do permanent damage to the slave (for example, damage an eye or knock out a tooth), then the slave would be released, as this would likely indicate that the master was beating him about the head, suggesting that more than discipline was intended.

Finally, we should address the matter of a daughter that was sold as a female slave (אָמָה *'amah*) in Exodus 21:7-11. Although the law required the release of the male slave after six years in Exodus 21:2 (and the release of both male and female slaves in Deuteronomy 15:17), a daughter who is sold specifically as a wife or concubine did not get released after six years. An Israelite could also take a wife from among the captives in war (Deut. 21:10-14). Both types of female slaves had the right to the status of wife, and could not simply be sold if they fell out of favor with their Israelite husband. If they were not provided for, they were to be either redeemed or set free.

There is obviously a great deal more that we can and will say about slavery in the Old Testament; however, this chapter is simply intended to provide a general introduction to what the sources tell us about the laws concerning the practice of slavery as portrayed in the Hebrew Bible. As we have seen, there were rules for Hebrew slaves that differed from foreign slaves, as Israelites could only be taken for a set period of time, and (at least by the time of Leviticus) could not be treated as proper slaves, but only as hired workers. Foreigners, on the other hand, could be treated as genuine slaves, kept for life, passed on as inheritance, and were not subject to the laws of release. Slaves were expected to be beaten as a form of discipline, but were not to be purposefully abused; should this overt abuse take place (evidenced by the loss of a tooth or damage to an eye), they were to be set free, owing nothing to the master. Slaves could be purchased both locally and abroad, and fathers could sell their daughters as female slaves to become the concubines or wives of their masters or his sons. In the coming chapters, we will examine more detailed aspects of Old Testament slavery, particularly in light of the cultural context of the ancient Near East.

# CHAPTER TWO:

# Slavery in the Ancient Near East: An Overview

As with many discussions concerning the Old Testament, one of the missing ingredients in the conversation is the context in which the biblical texts were written; this includes both the contexts of Israel, and the wider ancient Near East. There were many customs and traditions that formed the background for the laws and practices concerning slavery in the Hebrew Bible. These contexts also motivated and shaped the biblical laws as we see them in the legal texts. It would be unwise, therefore, to engage in a discussion about Old Testament slavery without understanding – to the greatest extent possible – the legal traditions of the societies that made up ancient Israel's cultural context.

The goal of this chapter will be to introduce the reader to the legal traditions that existed before and during the biblical period in the ancient Near East, with a particular focus on laws and practices regarding slavery. I will begin by providing a brief and general introduction to ancient Near

Eastern law, highlighting certain aspects and issues that will be important for our discussion. We will then identify the sources that are available from the ancient Near East that we can use to identify these legal traditions, including the so-called "law codes," legal documents, and texts from other genres (e.g., literary texts, proverbs, etc.). We will look at how these sources can be used, and how the information that we glean from them concerning slavery can inform our understanding of the practice as recorded in the Old Testament. Finally, we will turn to the practice of slavery itself and attempt to describe the laws that concern slavery, along with a consideration of its practical application. This will not only allow us to draw comparisons between ancient Near East and Old Testament slavery, but it will create an interpretive framework with which we can correctly understand the laws and practices in the Hebrew Bible.

There are many resources available for the detailed study of the reality and practice of slavery (and other aspects of law) in the ancient Near East, including Israel. A foundational resource that can be used by the non-specialist is Raymond Westbrook's 2003 two-volume edited work *A History of*

*Ancient Near Eastern Law.*[16] In this publication, scholars from the fields of Egyptology, Assyriology, Hittiteology, and Hebrew Bible come together to provide thorough summaries of the various aspects of law in the ancient Near East. This monumental work will be referenced often in this chapter and throughout the book, and the reader is encouraged to make use of this and other similar resources when studying legal issues in the ancient Near East.

Before we discuss the legal system, we should identify what we mean by the ancient Near East, both geographically and chronologically. Geographically, it will be useful to adopt Westbrook's definition, who identifies the region as "an area situated in what is now called the Middle East, extending from Iran to Egypt, and concentrated in an arc of territories sometimes known as the Fertile Crescent."[17] From a chronological standpoint, scholars generally consider this period to run from roughly 3000 to 330 BCE (from around the

---

[16] See the bibliography for the full citation, along with other books and articles on law and slavery.

[17] Westbrook 2003a: 2.

invention of writing to the conquest of Alexander the Great
and the Hellenization of the area).

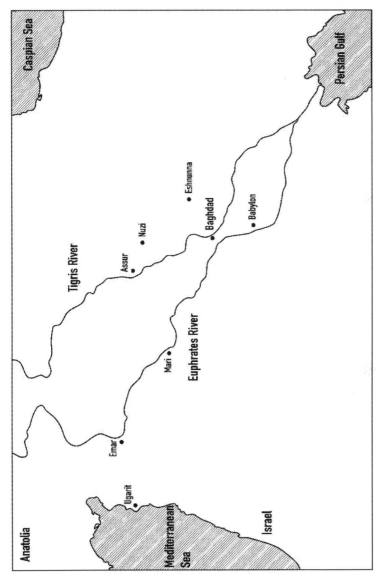

Map showing the locations mentioned in this book.
Modern city of Baghdad shown for context.

Given these rather wide geographical and chronological boundaries, you might wonder if we should even be talking about a single or consistent "legal tradition." Laws and legal customs change so frequently in our modern age; how could there have been any consistency over such a long period of time and in different areas of the Middle East? What we should bear in mind here, however, is that things change for us today much more rapidly and with greater frequency than thousands of years ago. Again, to cite Westbrook:

> "Modern law changes at a frenetic pace, but only in a desperate attempt to keep up with the pace of technological, economic, social, and ideological changes in society as a whole . . . Different conditions prevailed in the ancient Near East."[18]

Does that mean that every law and every tradition were the same throughout time and in every region? Of course not. However, as we will see, there seem to have been traditions during these periods that remained relatively constant over

---

[18] Ibid., 22.

the millennia, which can be seen in the varying regions through time.[19]

Let's talk about ancient Near Eastern law in general. Of course, a small section in a single chapter can hardly do justice to the complexities of the ancient Near Eastern legal system, but I will attempt to outline some of its more important features for our purposes.

When we consider our laws and overall legal system today, we generally think of a set of rules or regulations that we must abide by. We have laws and statutes that are well documented, and we appeal to them when determining the legality of a particular action. If Johnny steals a car, there are laws on the books that identify the illegality of that action, as well as the range of punishments that are required or enforceable. Thus, in our legal system, lawyers will cite

---

[19] Ibid., 4. "I would argue that all the ancient Near Eastern systems belonged in varying degrees to a common legal culture, one very different from any that obtains today. At the very least, they shared a legal ontology: a way of looking at the law that reflected their view of the world and determined the horizon of the lawmaker." For an overview of variant theories on the similarities and differences between the laws across these regions and periods, see Wells and Magdalene 2009: xiii-xvi.

previous cases where the courts have determined that X is illegal, for example, and those decisions inform the outcome of the case before a presiding judge. These types of codified laws are referred to as *civil law*. Those judging the facts of a case look to fixed laws, codes, and statutes to make their verdicts.

However, this type of civil law has not always been in place. During much of the history of the ancient Near East, it appears that judges were given much greater freedom when making their decisions. They did not think about their legal process in the same way that we do today. There were no fixed codes or statutes to which a judge would always appeal.[20] For example, writing about the oft-debated "Code" of Hammurabi, Bottéro argues:

---

[20] That is not to say that judges never looked back to previous decisions to determine their verdicts. It was much more complicated. Ibid., 14. "There is some evidence that previous decisions were regarded as a source of law. In the epilogue to his law code, Hammurabi advises one who is wronged to consult the list of his 'just judgments' on the stele so as to know his rights." However, Westbrook states, "Much of the law applied by the courts was probably customary law, derived not from known cases but from timeless tradition."

"Let us not lose sight of the 'Code' itself. If it collects in fact *verdicts of justice*, it establishes by that very fact the existence of a system of justice. It is only that the people did not have the same point of view as we have – just as they did not have the same idea of science as we do."[21]

This type of law – where judges are given freedom to develop rules and regulations – is known as *common law*. These so-called "law codes" were most likely not a form of normative legislation, but were the product of the legal tradition that stood behind them.[22] When we turn to the ancient Near Eastern legal texts, therefore, we need to bear all of this in

---

[21] Bottéro 1992: 179.

[22] Westbrook 2009a: 95. "In conclusion, it should be stressed that the importance of the cuneiform law codes must not be underestimated. They represent a considerable intellectual achievement, and as such made a vital contribution to the process that led to the law codes of late antiquity and thence to modern western statutes. At the same time, if we are to interpret their provisions correctly, their limitations should be recognized. *The most salient of these is that they were not normative legislation.*" [emphasis mine]

mind. It was likely not common legal practice to refer to case law when rendering judgments.

So, what kinds of sources do we have for understanding the legal system in the ancient Near East, particularly when it comes to slavery? Most of us are aware of the Law Code of Hammurabi, but there are several texts like it from different periods:[23]

> Laws of Ur-Namma - 2100 BCE
>
> Laws of Lipit-Ishtar - 1900 BCE
>
> Laws of Eshnunna - 1770 BCE
>
> Laws of Hammurabi - 1750 BCE
>
> Middle Assyrian Laws - 14th century BCE
>
> Hittite Laws - 16th - 12th centuries BCE
>
> Neo-Babylonian Laws - 7th century BCE

While many of us are more familiar with these law "codes," they are certainly not the only sources of legal information. I will discuss the sources here only very briefly, but will return to some of them in the remainder of this book.[24] Westbrook

---

[23] Westbrook 2003a: 9.

[24] Ibid., 4-12 for a thorough discussion of the sources.

lists several types of textual sources: royal decrees and instructions (to individuals), trial records, law codes, lexical texts (which contain legal vocabulary), transactional records, letters, historiographical documents, and literature. Each source must be evaluated as to the amount of bias or propaganda that it might contain, and whether it directly or indirectly refers to a particular legal custom. The majority of our documentation concerning the legal tradition comes from Mesopotamia, as opposed to other parts of the ancient Near East, because of the Mesopotamian tradition of writing on durable clay tablets that survive well in the archaeological record.

## The Laws and Practice of Ancient Near East Slavery

As in chapter one, the primary goal of this summary is to provide the reader with a substantial overview of slavery as we know it from the ancient Near East. As mentioned above, because our source material comes primarily from Mesopotamia, the evidence will lean that direction; however, if we are aware of this imbalance of evidence, we can at least keep this "bias" in mind as we interpret the data.

There are three primary aspects of slavery that I would like to focus in on:

1) Types of slavery, and how one becomes a slave.
2) Rights and legal standing of slaves.
3) Information concerning foreigners with respect to slavery.

By addressing these three aspects of slavery, we will set ourselves up to make a solid comparison between the laws and practices in the ancient Near East and those that are seen in the Old Testament.

*Debt- and Chattel-Slavery*

As in the Old Testament, there are generally two types of slavery that appear: debt-slavery and chattel-slavery. Debt-slaves were often those who had taken out a loan (or, more frequently, their family members) but were unable to pay back that loan to their creditor. The borrower, or one (or more) of their family members, were taken as a debt-slave by the creditor until the loan was repaid. Westbrook writes concerning debt-slaves during the Old Babylonian Period (ca. 2000-1600 BCE):

"Debt slaves were free persons who had
entered slavery by reason of debt . . . They
were alienable, but their slavery was
conditional upon the existence of the debt and
would be terminated with its extinction, for
whatever reason. Chattel slaves were slaves
who had entered slavery on any other basis
and whose slavery was in theory permanent
and unconditional."[25]

A specific case of such seizure can be seen during the first
half of the third millennium BCE, a time known as the Early
Dynastic Period. Claus Wilcke identifies one such seizure in
the textual evidence: "Note the exclamation of a defaulter,
"'let them take away the area of the Inana irrigation-ditch,
but let them not lead away my children!'"[26]

---

[25] Westbrook 2003b: 380. Both Westbrook and Mendehlson 1978: 15-16
cite YOS 8 31, a slave-sale document; see in particular obv. 8-14: "For
their debt one-third mina of silver, as their full price, he has paid. He who
brings a claim against them one mina of silver will pay."
[26] Wilcke 2003: 160. An edition of the text can be found in Wilcke 1996:
56-58 (grand document juridique, K).

While debt-slavery was technically a temporary condition, chattel-slavery tended to be permanent. For example, a person could become a chattel-slave by birth, through purchase, or as a war captive. In addition, debt-slaves could often become chattel-slaves if they were not redeemed within a specified period of time. For example, during the Old Assyrian Period (early 2nd millennium BCE), Veenhof observes:

> "Most slaves owned by Assyrians in Assur and in Anatolia seem to have been (originally) debt slaves – free persons sold into slavery by a parent, a husband, an elder sister, or by themselves . . . The possibility of redeeming a debt slave was limited in time, ranging from one month . . . to two . . . and perhaps even four years. As long as the people sold were debt slaves they enjoyed a certain protection, after that they could be sold by the creditor/owner 'where he liked,' even abroad."[27]

---

[27] Veenhof 2003: 449, who cites Balkan's edition of the Old Assyrian tablet kt a/k 250 (Balkan 1974: 31 [#14]).

The debt/chattel-slave distinction can also be seen in Nuzi. Zaccagnini observes:

> "Chattel slaves and their offspring could be the object of transfer and outright sale . . . Persons in debt servitude, that is, handed over as pledges in antichretic *tidennūtu* contracts, could not be sold or transferred to third parties."[28]

In short, during most of the periods of ancient Near Eastern history, one could become either a debt- or a chattel-slave, and the former could develop into the latter.

Captives of war were also a significant source for slavery in the ancient Near East. As in the Hebrew Bible, conquered peoples were often reduced to slavery. Beaulieu notes that during the Old Babylonian Period (ca. 2000-1600 B.C.E.), "Most slaves were either born in that status or came into it as prisoners of wars."[29] Similarly, concerning slavery in the Neo-Babylonian period, Dandamayev notes:

---

[28] Zaccagnini 2003: 586.

[29] Beaulieu 2018: 90.

"Turning prisoners of war into slaves was also
a widespread phenomenon. There was an
especially large number of such slaves in the
palace and temple households. There are
documents attesting to the sale of foreigners in
Babylonia after a successful campaign."[30]

While it may seem counterintuitive, as in Israel, much of
slavery in the ancient world was legally voluntary;
permission was often given, either by the one being enslaved,
or by the head of the household when giving his wife,
children, or slaves as a pledge.

"A citizen could not be enslaved against his
will if independent or without the permission
of the person under whose authority he was . . .
Although in practice economic circumstances
would often force a person into slavery, in law
his act was, strictly speaking, voluntary."[31]

As far as the law was concerned, individuals could not
generally be taken against their will. Those who defaulted on

---

[30] Dandamayev 1984: 107.

[31] Westbrook 2003a: 42.

loans and pledged themselves to a creditor, or those pledged who were under the debtor's control, were seen as entering slavery voluntarily. It is interesting to note, however, that this "permission" was at times (at least) an impossibility. At the city of Emar, for example, Westbrook notes:

> "Many of the documents emphasize that the transaction is voluntary (*ištu ramānišu*). This applies not only to self-sale but also to those who are the object of sale, although their consent must sometimes have been fictional, as in the case of a nursing infant (Emar 83)."[32]

Debt slavery was a significant source of slave creation during much of ancient Near Eastern history. Concerning the Early Dynastic and Sargonic Periods, Wilcke writes, "The majority of published slave sale documents record the creation of slavery rather than resale. Nearly a third deal with the creation of slavery by family members."[33] This was also the case during the Old Assyrian Period, as noted by Veenhof: "Most slaves owned by Assyrians in Assur and in Anatolia

---

[32] Westbrook 2003c: 665.

[33] Wilcke 2003: 159.

seem to have been (originally) debt slaves – free persons sold into slavery by a parent, a husband, an elder sister, or by themselves."[34]

Comparing recorded cases in the Hebrew Bible to what we see in the ancient Near Eastern documents, Mendehlson summarizes:

> "Cases of outright sale of children into slavery
> by their parents are not recorded in the Old
> Testament. However, the fact that parents sold
> their young girls into conditional slavery
> (Exod. 21:7-11), that creditors seized the
> children of their deceased debtors (II Kings
> 4:1), and that debt-ridden farmers were forced
> by law to hand their sons and daughters over
> as slaves (Neh. 5:5) show that, as in the
> neighboring countries of Babylonia and
> Assyria, Palestinians, when hard pressed,

---

[34] Veenhof 2003: 449.

could and probably did sell their children
'voluntarily' into servitude."[35]

### Slaves' Rights and Legal Standing

One of the aspects of slavery in the ancient world that people
often struggle with is the fact that slaves were the property
of their masters (to greater or lesser degrees), while at the
same time possessed rights and legal standing in their
societies. Many find it difficult to believe that a slave could
be considered property, and yet have rights under the law, as
these seem to be mutually exclusive. Nevertheless, both were
a reality under the legal system. In this section, we will
examine the evidence for slaves being owned as property, yet
having legal capacity, as well as certain protections and
rights under the law.

"Although slaves were regarded as property that could be
sold, hired, pledged, and inherited, they were accorded some
legal standing."[36] As in the Hebrew Bible, we find in the
ancient Near East that slaves were considered the property
of the owner, and could be bought, sold, inherited, and

---

[35] Mendehlson 1978: 10.

[36] Lafont and Westbrook 2003: 199.

disciplined – to varying degrees – depending on the type of slavery in question. In most historical periods, when a debtor defaulted on a loan and pledged himself or a family member to his creditor, the pledge was considered the slave of the creditor, but not strictly his property.

Certain laws and restrictions applied that did not apply to a proper chattel slave. Westbrook writes:

> "Debtors could give themselves or persons under their authority to creditors by way of pledge. The resulting conditions were analogous to those of slavery: the pledge lost his personal freedom and was required to serve the pledgee, who exploited the pledge's labor. Nonetheless, the relationship between debtor and creditor remained one of contract, not property. Since the pledgee did not own the pledge, he could not alienate him, nor did the pledge's property automatically vest in the pledgee."[37]

---

[37] Westbrook 2009b: 167.

Here we see an important legal distinction that must be taken into account when analyzing the status of slaves in the ancient world: we must determine in any given circumstance whether a slave fell under *family law* or *property law*.[38] When family law applied, the slave was treated as a person, while under property law, they were considered chattel.

Although slaves were often considered chattel – whether practically or legally – this did not mean that they were merely subject to the whims of their master, to be treated in any way that the master saw fit. As we saw in the Hebrew Bible, slaves had certain rights, and there were limitations on how they could be treated. For example, in the Old Testament, slaves were to have the right to rest on the Sabbath (Exod. 20:10; 23:12; Deut. 5:14) and were to be circumcised in order to be able to participate in various aspects of the cult (Exod. 12:44; Deut. 12:12, 18; Lev. 22:11). In addition, the slave had the right to be free from excessive beatings and outright abuse, and could not be killed with premeditation by the master (Exod. 21:20-21; 26-27). Similar

---

[38] Westbrook 2003a: 43.

types of rights and limitations existed in the laws of the ancient Near East.

In the Laws of Hammurabi, for example, law 117 stipulates that a debt-slave had the right to release after three years of service, compared to release after six years in the Hebrew Bible:

> "If an obligation is outstanding against a man and he sells or gives into debt service his wife, his son, or his daughter, they shall perform service in the house of their buyer or of the one who holds them in debt service for three years; their release shall be secured in the fourth year."[39]

If a man took a slave as a wife, laws 170-171 gave rights to the slave wife, providing her with freedom following the death of her master, including the right to continue to live in the estate, and perhaps even an equal portion of the master's property after his death.

---

[39] Roth 1997: 103.

"If a man's first-ranking wife bears him children and his slave woman bears him children, and the father during his lifetime then declares to (or: concerning) the children whom the slave woman bore to him, 'My children,' and he reckons them with the children of the first-ranking wife – after the father goes to his fate, the children of the first-ranking wife and the children of the slave woman shall equally divide the property of the paternal estate; the preferred heir is a son of the first-ranking wife, he shall select and take a share first. But if the father during his lifetime should not declare to (or: concerning) the children whom the slave woman bore to him, 'My children,' after the father goes to his fate, the children of the slave woman will not divide the property of the paternal estate with the children of the first-ranking wife. The release of the slave woman and of her children shall be secured; the children of the first-ranking wife will not make claims of slavery against the children of the slave woman. The first-ranking wife shall take her dowry and the

marriage settlement which her husband
awarded to her in writing, and she shall
continue to reside in her husband's dwelling;
as long as she is alive she shall enjoy the use of
it, but she may not sell it; her own estate shall
belong (as inheritance) only to her own
children."
(LH 170-171)[40]

More generally, during the last century of the third
millennium – the Ur III Period – slaves were allowed to
conduct their own cases in court, calling witnesses and giving
testimony, while during the New Kingdom in Egypt, slaves
could not only give evidence in court, but could also own
fields.[41] In fact, it was often the case that slaves were found
leading lives that were relatively well-off, practically
speaking. For example, Dandamayev observes, "In the Neo-
Babylonian period slaves were permitted to live as families,
and their natural reproduction from generation to generation

---

[40] Ibid., 113-114.

[41] Lafont and Westbrook 2003: 199; Jasnow 2003: 321.

had great significance, being the major source for replenishing the number of slaves."[42]

It is also important to establish that one's status as a slave did not entitle the master to mistreat or abuse them in any way that he wished. As we saw in the Hebrew Bible, there were limitations built into the law in an attempt to protect the slave from outright abuse. The same was true in the wider ancient Near East. For example, in the Laws of Hammurabi (115-116), the text reads:

> "If a man has a claim of grain or silver against another man, distrains a member of his household, and the distrainee dies a natural death while in the house of her or his distrainer, that case has no basis for a claim. If the distrainee should die from the effects of a beating or other physical abuse while in the house of her or his distrainer, the owner of the distrainee shall charge and convict his merchant, and if (the distrainee is) the man's son, they shall kill his (the distrainer's) son; if

---

[42] Dandamayev 1984: 107.

the man's slave, he shall weigh and deliver 20

shekels of silver; moreover, he shall forfeit

whatever he originally gave as the loan."[43]

Thus, if a member of a debtor's household is taken by a creditor, and the creditor beats and kills them, the creditor is to be held accountable for his actions. Similarly, in law 282 we read, "If a slave should declare to his master, 'You are not my master,' he (the master) shall bring charge and proof against him that he is indeed his slave, and his master shall cut off his ear."[44] While the slave was certainly able to be punished for attempting to lie his way out of service, the master was required to take the slave before the judges and prove that he was indeed his slave. He could not simply take it upon himself to beat and maim the slave. Westbrook notes:

> "Ironically, this [law] suggests limits on the
> owner's right to discipline his slave, since he is
> allowed to inflict only a specific punishment
> and only after proof of his slave's status in
> court. A letter from Mari reports that an owner

[43] Roth 1997: 103.

[44] Ibid., 132.

gouged out the eyes of his runaway slave but
could not execute him without an order from
the king."[45]

Another clear example of specific limitations on the physical
punishment of slaves can be seen in the *Middle Assyrian
Palace Decrees*.[46] These regulations concern palace personnel
– particularly women – as well as issues surrounding their
activities in the palace. Paragraph 18 reads:

"[Ashur-dan, overseer, son of Ninurta-apil-
Ekur,] himself also overseer, issued a decree
for his palace personnel: Either a wife of the
king [or any other palace woman – if her slave
woman] commits [a punishable offense against
her mistress, . . . or should commit any
misdeed, either [the wife of the king] or the
palace woman whose slave woman committed
a punishable offense against her shall strike
her 30 blows with rods. [... If the slave woman]
who was beaten (by her mistress for her first

---

[45] Westbrook 2003b: 383.
[46] Roth 1997: 195-209.

offense) [...] commits a (second) punishable offense against her mistress . . . her mistress shall bring her [before the king]; in the presence of the king, they shall impose upon her the punishment which he shall determine; [...] a second time he shall give (the slave woman back) to her mistress. If the palace woman [whose slave woman] she beat in accordance with [the royal decree ... is excessive and the slave] dies from the blows, or to [..., the palace woman] who has killed her slave woman [shall suffer] for her insolence; she [is held responsible for] a punishable offense against the king."[47]

The situation described above involves a slave woman who had done something offensive or punishable to her mistress. The mistress was permitted to beat her slave for the first offense. However, should the female slave commit a second offense, the mistress was to take the slave before the king, who would dispense judgment upon the slave. The text

---

[47] Ibid., 203-204.

explains that 1) the mistress must obtain the king's permission to punish the slave a second time, and 2) if the mistress beat the slave woman so that she died, the mistress would be held responsible for that death, having committed a punishable offense. Magdalene, et al. concur:

> "If the sentence involves beating, but the
> mistress beats the slave excessively and kills
> her, the mistress 'will bear the guilt of (an
> offense against) the king' . . . The mistress
> possesses the right to beat her slave, in light of
> the king's authorization, but exceeding the
> allowed level of punishment means that she
> has failed to comply with the instructions of
> the royal court."[48]

Not only were there laws in place to protect slaves from excessive violence in a variety of circumstances, but by the first millennium BCE, the rules for slavery had apparently developed in Babylonia, particularly concerning the practice

---

[48] Magdalene, Wunsch, and Wells 2019: 191.

of debt slavery. Dandamayev writes concerning the Neo-Babylonian Period:

> "Debt slavery was not widespread at this time
> and was no longer of great significance.
> Besides, the creditor could no longer sell a
> debtor into slavery to a third person. Usually
> the debtor paid off the loan by *antichresis* (free
> work for the creditor), thereby preserving his
> freedom."[49]

In short, just because a slave was considered the property of the master, or had been seized or pledged for defaulting on a loan, this did not entitle the master to treat the slave in any way that he wished. Slaves, both debt and chattel, were accorded certain rights and protections under ancient Near Eastern law.

*Protection of Foreigners*

There is no question that the Old Testament calls for the care and protection of the weak and underprivileged, including (perhaps most notably) the resident alien. As with

---

[49] Dandamayev 1992: 59.

other aspects of the laws found in the Old Testament, however, this was not unique to the Hebrew Bible. In fact, it was a common theme found in ancient Near Eastern legal texts. The foreigner was considered to be particularly vulnerable, both because of the distance that he had traveled from his homeland, as well as his possible or likely ignorance of the customs and practices of the nation in which he was (temporarily) residing. Thus, the law took certain steps to prevent the foreigner from being abused or mistreated.

By way of example, in Mesopotamia, during the early part of the second millennium (the Old Babylonian Period), the Laws of Eshnunna made provisions to protect the foreigner from unfair treatment. In law 41 we read, "If a foreigner, a *napṭaru*, or a *mudû* wishes to sell his beer, the woman innkeeper shall sell the beer for him at the current rate."[50] Westbrook comments on this law, "A foreigner could acquire a protected status from the local ruler and thus become a resident alien (*ubarum*). LE 41 protects the resident alien

---

[50] Roth 1997: 65.

along with other categories of outsider from economic exploitation by a taverness."[51]

Moving forward to the latter part of the second millennium, during the Middle Babylonian Period, Slanski writes:

> "A *narû* passage reads: 'Whensoever in the future, be he Elamite, or Subarian, or Amorite, or Akkadian, officer, magistrate, who would come forward and litigate...' This passage suggests that any of those persons so identified had access to the legal system. Most *narûs* prohibit ordering a foreigner or a stranger to violate the monument . . . Sanction for violating the monument is to fall upon the native-born person who would take advantage of a foreigner's ignorance in order to violate the entitlement."[52]

Finally, concerning the laws in Ugarit, near the end of the second millennium, Rowe notes:

---

[51] Westbrook 2003b: 377.

[52] Slanski 2003: 497 (L. 7076).

"Resident aliens were members of the
community . . . they did enjoy most of the
rights and obligations of citizenship, such as
owning land . . . Foreign visiting agents (*ubru*)
and *ḥapiru*'s also enjoyed a protected status,
namely, the hospitality of the king, but were
hardly subject to domestic law."[53]

We see, therefore, that the protection of resident foreigners
was a common theme in the ancient Near East, and its
presence in the laws found in Mesopotamia, Ugarit, and the
Hebrew Bible should come as no surprise to us; this would
have been part of the common legal tradition of the region.

## Conclusion

This chapter contains a very brief overview of the general
nature of both the legal traditions in the ancient Near East,
and the practice of slavery. The position that we have taken
in this chapter is that, although the laws in the various
nations and time periods were often distant from one another
– both geographically as well as chronologically – there was a
common legal tradition that remained relatively consistent

---

[53] Rowe 2003: 723.

throughout the periods under investigation. We surveyed the general nature of ancient Near Eastern law, including the law "codes" and how they should be understood in their contexts. We then described the general nature of slavery, including the distinction between debt- and chattel-slavery. We saw that, as far as the law was concerned, much of the slavery that was practiced was considered voluntary, even if a slave was seized by a creditor for failure to repay a debt.

We also saw that slaves were often considered property or were under the direct control of the master; however, this did not entitle the master to treat the slave in any way that he wished. While physical discipline was expected, there were limits placed upon the master. Certain punishments required judicial sanction; yet even these were limited in their scope. Slaves were also accorded certain rights under the law, and their legal status often granted them rights that we might not expect, including testifying in court and calling witnesses. Slaves could own land, make transactions, and often operated much as a free person might. Finally, we examined what the law required concerning the treatment of foreigners, including resident aliens, observing that they were to be protected, to varying degrees, from abuse and mistreatment by local citizens. This care, we will see, also appears in the Hebrew Bible. In summation, when we compare the nature of slavery in the Hebrew Bible to that obtaining in the ancient Near East, we quickly see that, while there are certain distinctions, there is an overall commonality between these systems, suggesting that the laws of the Hebrew Bible were also part of the broader ancient Near Eastern legal tradition.

# CHAPTER THREE:

# Commentary on Slavery Passages in the Hebrew Bible

To this point, we have surveyed the essential aspects of slavery in both the Hebrew Bible and the wider ancient Near East. In this chapter, we will examine the major passages in the Old Testament legal texts that concern the appropriate practice of slavery. While information can be gleaned from other portions of the Hebrew Bible, the most frequently cited and significant passages are Exodus 21, Leviticus 25, and Deuteronomy 15. We will also address Deuteronomy 20, as the regulations for the practice of warfare have had some bearing on the discussion about slavery. The goal in this chapter will be to properly examine these passages in their biblical and ancient Near Eastern contexts in order to identify the principles they contain that relate to slavery. While we will not deal with every facet of these passages (there are many excellent commentaries that perform that function quite well), we will address the more significant portions that concern the discussion of slavery.

## Exodus 21

Perhaps one of the most significant chapters cited in the discussion on slavery in the Hebrew Bible is Exodus 21, which represents the first section of the so-called "Covenant Code" (Exod. 21-23). The Covenant Code is generally considered to be the earliest of the three major legal sections that deal with slavery (Exod. 21, Deut. 15, and Lev. 25).[54] In Exodus 21, we see laws concerning Hebrew debt-slavery, the manumission of Hebrew slaves, the Hebrew maidservant, the treatment of slaves, and repayment for harm caused to a slave.

*Hebrew Debt-Slave or Foreigner?*

Let's begin our discussion by asking the question, "Is this passage describing a Hebrew debt-slave for a foreign slave?" Here are the opening verses of Exodus 21:

> "These are the laws you are to set before them:
> If you buy a Hebrew servant, he is to serve you
> for six years. But in the seventh year, he shall

---

[54] For an excellent introduction to the various theories of dating and composition of the Pentateuch, see Collins 2018: 53-69.

go free, without paying anything. If he comes
alone, he is to go free alone; but if he has a wife
when he comes, she is to go with him. If his
master gives him a wife and she bears him
sons or daughters, the woman and her children
shall belong to her master, and only the man
shall go free. But if the servant declares, 'I love
my master and my wife and children and do
not want to go free,' then his master must take
him before the judges. He shall take him to the
door or the doorpost and pierce his ear with an
awl. Then he will be his servant for life"
(Exod. 21:1-6).

This passage begins with the laws regarding the "Hebrew
slave" (עֶבֶד עִבְרִי *eved 'ivri*). This phrase has posed some
interpretive difficulties for scholars in the field, particularly
with respect to the word *'ivri*, "Hebrew." Part of the
discussion has focused on the apparent similarities between
the word *'ivri* and a word that was used to describe groups of
outsiders or outlaws, which appears in other ancient Near
Eastern texts: *ḫabiru*. There have been several attempts to
connect the *ḫabiru* found in the 2nd millennium (in
particular) – for example, the *ḫabiru* known from Nuzi (see

below) – to the term *'ivri* found in Exodus 21.[55] Dozeman writes:

> "Scholars have sought to relate the word 'Hebrew' to Akkadian *ha-pi-ru* (Sumerian SA.GAZ), a reference to fugitives and outlaws in the ancient Near East. But continued research has made a direct connection between the word 'Hebrew' and 'Hapiru' unlikely."[56]

But outside of the apparent similarities between these words, why would a connection between *'ivri* and *ḫabiru* be of any significance?

Traditionally, the word *'ivri* has been understood as a "gentilic," or a term that refers to an individual's nationality or ethnicity. Understood in this way, the term *'ivri* would

---

[55] Zaccagnini 2003: 585-586. "A somewhat different case is that of male and female foreigners (including persons from Assur and Babylonia), called *ḫapiru* ('immigrants, refugees'), who gave themselves in slavery (*ardūtu*) to private individuals or the palace administration. Poverty was the cause of these agreements, whose juridical features require further analysis."

[56] Dozeman 2009: 76.

have referred to a "Hebrew" – a member of that ethnic group. However, among the texts that were discovered at the ancient city of Nuzi, we find a group of people known as the *ḥabiru*. These individuals were not citizens of Nuzi, and were usually foreigners, who would bind themselves to citizens as slaves in order to have their needs met by their masters. Because these *ḥabiru* were usually foreigners, and the words *ʿivri* and *ḥabiru* seem so similar, it was hypothesized by some that these *ʿivri* were not "Hebrews," but were instead *foreigners* who were selling themselves to Israelites as slaves. If these *ʿivri* were foreigners, then the laws in this section of Exodus 21 would be in conflict with the well-known law seen in Leviticus 25, where foreigners were able to be purchased and owned for life. This would call for a reevaluation of Leviticus 25 and its laws concerning foreign slaves. Jackson comments on the significance of this interpretation: "If, then, we use the comparative evidence to illuminate the meaning of *ʿivri* in *Exodus*, the *ḥabiru* interpretation leads to the conclusion that this law envisages the protection of foreign slaves, the very opposite of the traditional view."[57]

---

[57] Jackson 2006: 80.

While this connection might seem attractive in light of the texts from Nuzi, there are several seemingly insurmountable problems with understanding the *'ivri* in Exodus 21 as foreigners. First, and foremost, is the way that the term *'ivri* is used in the Hebrew Bible. It appears in the Joseph story, for example, clearly referring to the nationality of Joseph during his time in Egypt (e.g., Gen. 39:14, 17; 40:15; 41:12; 43:32). We also see this usage in the early chapters of Exodus, when the Hebrew women are contrasted with the Egyptian women. See, for example, Exodus 1:19: "The midwives answered Pharaoh, '*Hebrew* women are not like *Egyptian* women; they are vigorous and give birth before the midwives arrive'" (emphasis mine).

Of course, words can take on different shades of meaning, depending on how they are used in a particular context. However, when we view the use of the term *'ivri* in the legal passages of the Hebrew Bible, it becomes clear that the word is used specifically to refer to fellow Israelites, even appearing in parallel with the word "brother." For example, in Deuteronomy 15:12 – one of the three major legal passages about slavery – the text reads, "If your brother, a male Hebrew or female Hebrew, should be sold to you, then he will work for you six years, and in the seventh year you will send

71

him away from you free."[58] I have translated the Hebrew phrase that means "your brother, a male Hebrew or female Hebrew" a bit woodenly; however, I have rendered it in this way so that the reader can see the juxtaposition of the words "your brother" and "male Hebrew or female Hebrew." The NET smooths out the translation: "If your fellow Hebrew – whether male or female…" The material point is that "your brother" stands in parallel to the term *'ivri* in both the masculine and feminine forms, indicating that this is a fellow Israelite.

Kline notes concerning this verse:

> "The biblical law is patently not dealing with
> foreign servants but with those who were their
> masters' brethren. The Deut. 15:12 expansion
> of the original statement reads, 'If thy brother
> a Hebrew man, or a Hebrew woman, be sold to
> thee'; while Jeremiah, further expanding it
> urges 'that every man should let go free his
> man-servant and every man his maid-servant,
> that is a Hebrew or Hebrewess; that none

---

[58] My translation.

should make bondmen of them, namely, of a Jew, his brother' (34:9, cf. vs. 14). While one may then recognize the instructive parallels in the conditions of servanthood at Nuzu and in the biblical legislation, **it is impossible to hold that *'Ibri* is in this legislation a technical term for a specific type of servanthood and least of all for the idea of 'foreign-servant'. Its usage is rather ethnic, as always.**" [emphasis mine][59]

In short, although the term *'ivri* appears in some ways to – at least in form – partially compare to the term *ḥabiru*, the way that the word *'ivri* is used in the biblical texts makes its meaning very clear. We cannot read into these passages the meaning "foreigner" if the context does not warrant or allow for such a meaning. As we have seen, *'ivri* is used to not only identify the person as part of an ethnic group, but specifically the group of Israelites being discussed in the biblical legal texts. Propp summarizes this point well: "I admit that the *'ab/piru* connection is tantalizing and probably valid on some

---

[59] Kline 1958: 48-49.

level . . . But, regardless of etymology, in the Bible *'ibrî* 'Hebrew' functions as the ethnic term for an Israelite."[60]

Thus, it appears that Exodus 21:2-6 is not referring to a type of foreign slave (that is, a *ḥabiru*); instead, the passage is speaking specifically about the laws concerning slavery for an Israelite. So, the basic rule concerning Israelite debt-slaves in this section is that there is a distinct limit upon the length of time an Israelite could make a fellow Israelite serve as a slave: six years. In the seventh year, the owner is to set the slave free. But there are other aspects of this passage that should be addressed, including the purchasing of slaves and the distinction between the release of the male and female slaves.

### Purchasing Slaves

We should take a moment and discuss the word "buy" or "purchase" in Exodus 21:2. There has been some debate about whether we should translate this, "If you *buy* a Hebrew slave" or "If you *acquire* a Hebrew slave." In other words, I will often hear, "Doesn't the Hebrew word 'purchase' (קָנָה

---

*qanah*) simply mean 'acquire?' Doesn't that mean that we don't have to understand this as literally 'buying' people?" This type of logic also frequently extends to something like, "Aren't we just talking about 'buying' and 'selling' people in the same way that we 'buy' and 'sell' sports players today? We are just talking about buying their contracts, and not the individuals themselves."

There is no question that the use of the Hebrew word *qanah*, "buy", has a certain amount of fluidity and flexibility. However, when referencing property (which would include slaves, as we will see), the term often simply refers to purchasing in the normal sense, particularly by paying for the item with silver. Let's take a look at some examples. In Genesis 49:30 we read, "The cave in the field of Machpelah, near Mamre in Canaan, which Abraham bought (*qanah*) along with the field as a burial place from Ephron the Hittite." If we remember the story, Abraham purchased the cave and field in Genesis 23:16 for 400 shekels of silver. Here, the term *qanah* clearly refers to a typical transaction, in which silver is exchanged for the ownership rights to that piece of property. Another example can be seen in Jeremiah 13:2: "So I bought (*qanah*) a belt, as the Lord directed, and put it around my waist." Again, this is a typical purchase transaction. We see another example of this type of simple transaction in Jeremiah 19:1a: "This is what the Lord says: 'Go and buy (*qanah*) a clay jar from the potter.'"

In addition to things like land, belts, and clay jars being purchased, we see that slaves could also be bought; these were purchased, for example, by Abraham, the priests, and even the wealthy author of Ecclesiastes. For instance, in Genesis 17:12 we see, "For the generations to come every male among you who is eight days old must be circumcised, including those born in your household or bought with money (מִקְנַת־כֶּסֶף *miqnat kesef*) from a foreigner – those who are not your offspring." The phrase *miqnat kesef* literally means, 'a purchase of silver;' *miqnat* comes from the word *qanah* "to buy," and *kesef* means "silver." The same phrase appears in Exodus 12:44: "Any slave you have bought (lit. 'purchase of silver' (*miqnat kesef*) may eat it after you have circumcised him." We also see slaves being purchased in Leviticus 22:10-11: "No one outside a priest's family may eat the sacred offering, nor may the guest of a priest or his hired worker eat it. But if a priest buys a slave with money, or if slaves are born in his household, they may eat his food." Again, the text distinguishes between two types of slaves in this passage: those born in the house, and those purchased with money.

Finally, the author of Qohelet (Ecclesiastes) wrote of his great wealth in Ecclesiastes 2:7: "I bought male and female slaves and had other slaves who were born in my house. I also owned more herds and flocks than anyone in Jerusalem before me."

Concerning this use of the verb "to buy," Dozeman writes, "The verb 'to buy' indicates the act of purchase, not simply of slaves (Lev. 22:11; 25:44-45) but also of other commodities such as land (Gen. 25:10; 33:19)."[61] In addition, Seow notes other passages that describe such transactions: "The verb *qnh* is used for the buying of slaves (Gen. 39:1; 47:23; Amos 8:6; Neh. 5:8)."[62] Thus, it would be incorrect to assert that the verb *qanah*, "to buy, purchase, acquire", does not indicate the purchase of slaves in these passages simply because the verb *can* have the meaning "to acquire" in other places. Milgrom confirms:

> "The assumption here is that the alien is a chattel-slave, not a debt-slave. This is confirmed by the verb *qānâ* 'purchase.' A non-

---

[61] Dozeman 2009: 527.

[62] Seow 2008: 129.

> Israelite chattel-slave is defined as a *miqneh kesep* 'purchase' (Gen. 17:12-13, 23, 27; Exod. 12:44) or simply as *kaspô* 'his property' (Exod. 21:21). It is hardly an accident that *miqneh* also denotes 'livestock.'"[63]

It is clear, therefore, that we need not attempt to soften the word "purchase" by comparing it to buying and trading sports players today. Even with debt-slavery, there is obviously a much stronger ownership status for the master than with an owner or manager of an athlete today. As we will see, athletes do not work in the homes and/or in the fields for their owners, who are advised to beat them with wooden rods to keep them in line. They are not physically detained, and spouses are not given by the master only to be kept – along with their children – after the termination of the athlete's contract. To compare these two situations, in my opinion, is rather overly simplistic and looking for a way to minimize the reality and nature of slavery in the Hebrew Bible.

---

[63] Milgrom 2001: 2230.

*The Male Slave's Release*

We have seen that the slaves in Exodus 21:2-6 are almost certainly not foreigners, and that the language of "purchasing" should likely be understood in the common sense of buying with money. The text describes the laws for what would happen when a Hebrew slave, having served six years, would be set free. In the first scenario, the slave has come into his master's home either single (unmarried) or married. If he came in single, he will leave single. If he was married, his wife will also go with him. Simple enough. In v. 4, however, we see a second scenario: if the slave entered the master's service single, and the master gave the slave a wife during his six-year term of service, then the wife (and any children that she bore) would not go free; they would belong to the master.

We see a similar regulation in the Laws of Ur-Nammu (#4) from the late third millennium BCE: "If a male slave marries a female slave, his beloved, and that male slave (later) is given his freedom, she/he will not leave (or: be evicted from?)

the house."[64] Westbrook cites both Exodus 21 and the Laws of Ur-Nammu #4 when he notes:

> "Where a married couple were enslaved for
> debt, they would be released together, but if
> the master had given the slave a female slave
> of his own as a wife, property law prevailed
> and he would have to leave without her (Exod.
> 21:2-6; LU 4)."[65]

The obvious problem, of course, is how immoral this practice seems from our modern point of view. Indeed, this passage sometimes causes problems for certain Christians; some go to great lengths to give the rationale for God giving such laws. For example, concerning the choices facing the newly freed slave, Paul Copan writes:

> "1. He could wait for his wife and kids to finish
> their term of service while he worked
> elsewhere . . . Yet if the now free man worked
> elsewhere, this would mean (a) he would be

---

[64] Roth 1997: 17.
[65] Westbrook 2003a: 44.

separated from his family, and (b) his boss would no longer supply him with food, clothing, and shelter . . . 2. He could get a decent job elsewhere and save his shekels to pay his boss to release his wife and kids from contractual obligations . . . 3. He could commit himself to working permanently for his employer – a life contract (Exod. 21:5-6)."[66]

While this may seem like a logical approach to understanding the situation found in the text, the scenario described by Copan is likely one that did not exist. The husband did not go out with the knowledge that his wife and children would be released after their term of service. The law in Exodus 21:2-6 is concerned with his release, the different circumstances in which the slave could find himself, and the regulations that would apply in each situation. If the male slave was given a wife by the master, she would almost certainly have been a female slave. Her release was not required, nor the children's, as they would be considered houseborn slaves. Durham explains:

---

[66] Copan 2011: 138-139.

"If, however, his wife has married him during his servitude, obviously by the permission and through the provision of his owner, both the wife and any children born to such a union must remain with the owner when the 'temporary' slave claims his freedom of the seventh year. They are obviously the owner's property."[67]

Propp agrees, "A Hebrew maidservant is not released after six years . . . even if she is married to a Hebrew slave (21:4)."[68]

In other words, the male slave is not choosing between permanent slavery and leaving his wife and children temporarily, awaiting the day that he can either free them from their "contractual obligations" or until their term of service is up. Neither of the latter situations apply. The wife is almost certainly not a debt-slave, and their children are simply houseborn slaves. Neither the wife nor the children are expected to be released. Thus, the choice facing the male

---

[67] Durham 2015: 321.

[68] Propp 2006: 196-197.

slave is one of leaving behind his wife and children, or taking
an oath to serve his master in perpetuity:

> "But if the servant declares, 'I love my master
> and my wife and children and do not want to
> go free,' then his master must take him before
> the judges. He shall take him to the door or the
> doorpost and pierce his ear with an awl. Then
> he will be his servant for life"
> (Exod. 21:5-6).

Jackson summarizes:

> "After stating the basic rule of liberation *ex
> lege* after six years' service (Exod. 21:2), verses
> 3-6 deal with the effects upon the slave's
> family, taking account of two variables: the
> source of that family (pre-enslavement or post-
> enslavement, the 'wife' provided in the latter
> case by the master); and, if post-enslavement,
> whether the slave is prepared to abandon his
> new family."[69]

---

[69] Jackson 2006: 85.

*"Maidservant"*

Following the stipulations laid out concerning the male
Hebrew slave and his terms of service, the text moves to the
female slave: the "maidservant" (אָמָה *'amah*).

> "If a man sells his daughter as a servant, she is
> not to go free as male servants do. If she does
> not please the master who has selected her for
> himself, he must let her be redeemed. He has
> no right to sell her to foreigners, because he
> has broken faith with her. If he selects her for
> his son, he must grant her the rights of a
> daughter. If he marries another woman, he
> must not deprive the first one of her food,
> clothing and marital rights. If he does not
> provide her with these three things, she is to
> go free, without any payment of money."
> (Exod. 21:7-11).

Again, a general principle is explored, applying it to two
different scenarios. The law states that, unlike male slaves, if
a man sells his daughter as a female slave, she is not
released after a six-year term. Mendelsohn writes:

"In contrast to the Hebrew male slave who was
to be freed, according to Exodus 21:2 on the
seventh year, the Hebrew maiden who was
sold by her father was to remain in bondage
forever . . . and serve her master both as a
slave and as a concubine."[70]

Some will argue that, because the word "slave" (עֶבֶד *'eved*) can
be used to refer to both males and females, it is also
ambiguous here in Exodus 21:2. The passage would then
apply the seventh-year release to both male and female
slaves. However, there are several problems with this
interpretation. First, and perhaps foremost, is the language
of verses 7-11. The female slave is specifically *not* to be
released, contrasted with "as the male slaves" are. Second,
the use of "wife" in Exodus 21:3-5 makes it clear that this is a
male slave that has either already taken – or has been given
by his master – a wife. Concerning this, Jackson writes:

"But that does not mean that *Exod.* 21:2-6
should be interpreted as having female debt-
slaves also in mind (despite the fact that *eved*,

---

[70] Mendelsohn 1978: 42.

when used alone, can sometimes include a
female slave). *Exod.* 21:4 cannot apply to such
a female debt-slave, since it speaks of an *ishah*
given to him."[71]

So, the law requires the release of a male Hebrew slave after
six years, but not the release of a female slave; she is being
sold as a slave and concubine/wife to her master. This is
almost certainly the rationale behind the six-year law of
release not applying to her, as she is most likely being sold
into some form of sexual or marital relationship with her
master. Durham explains:

"The provisions here stipulated for such a
woman make it very likely that she was not
sold into slavery for general purposes, but only
as a bride, and therefore with provisions
restricting her owner-husband concerning her
welfare if he should become dissatisfied with
the union."[72]

---

[71] Jackson 2006: 88. The word *ishah* means "woman, wife" in Hebrew.
[72] Durham 2015: 322.

However, the law requires that, if the master loses his liking for her, he cannot sell her to a foreign nation, as she has moved out of the status of strictly a slave, and is thus to be accorded a measure of protection. Whether the master chooses her for himself, or for his son, she is to continue to receive those things that are due her (food, clothing, etc.). Failing this, the master must allow her to go free, without payment. Propp concludes:

> "While at first glance the nonliberation of the maidservant may seem oppressive, the statute is designed to *protect* her. Instead of liberating a menial to shift for herself, the law encourages the owner to elevate her to the status of wife or at least concubine."[73]

Even with this form of protection contained in the law, one could easily argue that this would be considered grossly immoral by today's standards. Selling one's daughter into slavery concubinage or marriage, while better than general slavery, would by no means be acceptable today. In response, some have argued that the female slave was an *agent* in this

---

[73] Propp 2006: 197.

"transaction," and that she *actively chose* to enter into this relationship. The Hebrew of Exodus 21:7, however, is clear and straightforward: the father *sells* his daughter; no agency is ascribed to the daughter. However, v. 8 is more complicated, and some have argued that the Greek translation of this verse seems to indicate that the daughter has chosen to go with her master. The Greek word καθωμολογήσατο (*kathomologesato*; an aorist middle indicative of καθομολογέω) is translated by some in v. 8 as "she betrothed herself." Thus, she would be an agent in the transaction, meaning that there would be no involuntary slavery present in the text.

There are several problems with this interpretation. First (and without going into great detail), the grammar of v. 8 does not seem to allow for the daughter to be the agent, as the relative pronoun ἥν *hen* (which references the daughter) is in the accusative case; she is not the subject of the verb. Muraoka writes concerning this verse, "aor. mid. . . . *to promise to give in marriage*: s father and + acc. pers. (daughter) and dat. pers. (male), ἥν αὐτῷ καθωμολογήσατο 'whom he [= the girl's father] had betrothed to him' Ex 21.8;

21.9."[74] More simply, what Muraoka is saying, is that the verb has the *father* as the subject, the *daughter* as the object, and the *master* as the person to whom the daughter is being betrothed. Thus, he translates this, "whom he [= the girl's father] had betrothed to him." Propp writes, "In 21:7, the subject is the girl's father not her purchaser . . . Exodus stresses rather the woman's passivity, subject to the authority first of her father and then of her purchaser."[75] Finally, he states:

> "With LXX-Aquila-Symmachus-Theodotion, I
> take the verb *ya'ad* as meaning 'to make a
> commitment,' in this case to elevate the
> maidservant into a concubine or wife . . . That
> is, the verb refers to the action of her guardian,
> who has the right to bestow her on whom he
> pleases . . . this includes the option of marrying
> her himself."[76]

---

[74] Muraoka 2009: 351.

[75] Propp 2006: 196.

[76] Ibid., 197.

In short, there is little to indicate that the daughter was in any way involved in the decision to sell herself to the master; as was the cultural norm, the decision was made for her.

To summarize, Exodus 21:7-11 presents the legal stipulations that surround the selling of one's daughter into slavery as a "maidservant" (אָמָה 'amah). If a father falls into debt, he may sell his daughter into slavery; however, certain provisions are made to protect her and her master in this transaction. First, she is not to be released after six years of service, as she is most likely not functioning as a simple slave, but as a concubine or wife. Second, if her master loses his liking for her, he may not simply change her status back to simple slavery and sell her to a foreign nation; he must allow her to be redeemed. If she remains, she is to be provided for; if her provisions are not maintained, she is to be set free. While these regulations provide a measure of protection for both the master and the woman, the woman was still a passive participant in the transaction.

*Kidnapping*

I would like to briefly touch upon Exodus 21:16, as this verse if often cited early in a conversation about slavery in the Old Testament as a defense of the practice. The text reads,

"Anyone who kidnaps someone is to be put to death, whether the victim has been sold or is still in the kidnapper's possession." This verse is regularly quoted in a debate, followed by the argument, "If it was illegal to steal a person, then slavery could not have existed. You couldn't take someone against their will, and if you volunteer to serve someone, then it is not slavery." While this might seem like an airtight argument, there are four things that we need to consider. First, the act of stealing another human being is in no way necessary for the practice of slavery as described in the Hebrew Bible. Second, the meaning of this verse is not as straightforward as we might expect. Third, this regulation not only existed in Israelite law, but also in the wider ancient Near East. Finally, slavery is not restricted to involuntary servitude, though involuntary servitude was certainly endorsed in the biblical laws.

While the mention of the word "slavery" often conjures up images of that which was practiced in the Antebellum South (including kidnapping), as we have seen, slavery in the Hebrew Bible should be defined on its own terms, and need not require the kidnapping of others to be classified as "slavery." As we will see in our analysis of Leviticus 25:44-46, those from foreign nations (both inside and outside of the land of Israel) were allowed to be purchased as permanent slaves. The issue that is articulated in Exodus 21:16 (and Deut. 24:7) deals with the unlawful procurement through theft of a free person in order to sell them into slavery. This in no way negates the lawful practice of slavery as described in the passages under discussion.

Now let's turn to the meaning of Exodus 21:16 itself. There is some debate concerning whether this verse refers to stealing *any* free person to reduce them to slavery, or if it simply refers to stealing an *Israelite*. Some of the confusion arises from a parallel legal text found in Deuteronomy 24:7, where the text reads, "If someone is caught kidnaping a fellow Israelite and treating or selling them as a slave, the kidnapper must die. You must purge the evil from among you." The law speaks only to the abduction of an Israelite, and not of a foreigner, despite the fact that resident foreigners are mentioned in several other places in Deuteronomy 24 (for example, verses 14, 17, and 19-22). Westbrook writes:

> "Involuntary enslavement applied only to
> foreigners. With respect to one's fellow
> citizens, the law codes contained stern

injunctions against kidnapping free persons for
the purpose of reducing them to slavery: CH
14: If a man steals the young son of a man, he
shall be killed. Exod 21:16: A man who steals a
man and sells him, and one in whose hand he
is found, shall be put to death. The safest
course was to sell the kidnap victim abroad, as
is illustrated by the story of Joseph."[77]

Even if we assume that kidnapping was illegal for both
citizen and foreigner alike, we need to understand that it was
also illegal to steal a citizen in the wider ancient Near East.
For example, as cited above, in the Laws of Hammurabi, #14,
we read, "If a man should kidnap the young child of another
man, he shall be killed."[78] Additionally, in the Hittite Laws,
#19-21, we read the following:

"If a Luwian abducts a free person, man or
woman, from the land of Hatti, and leads him
away to the land of Luwiya/Arzawa, and
subsequently the abducted person's owner

---

[77] Westbrook 2009b: 174.
[78] Roth 1997: 84.

recognizes him, the abductor shall bring (i.e. forfeit) his entire house. If a Hittite abducts a Luwian man in the land of Hatti itself, and leads him away to the land of Luwiya, formerly they gave 12 persons, but now he shall give 6 persons. He shall look to his house for it. If a Hittite man abducts a Hittite male slave from the land of Luwiya, and leads him here to the land of Hatti, and subsequently the abducted person's owner recognizes him, the abductor shall pay him 12 shekels of silver. He shall look to his house for it. If anyone abducts the male slave of a Luwian man from the land of Luwiya and brings him to the land of Hatti, and his owner later recognizes him, the owner shall only take back his own slave: there shall be no compensation."[79]

Propp observes, "In the Laws of Hammurapi, too, kidnapping is a capital offence . . . In the Hittite Laws (§§19-24), however, abduction may be compounded with a payment."[80]

---

[79] Ibid., 220.
[80] Propp 2006: 213.

Interestingly, by the middle of the first millennium BCE, during the Neo-Babylonian Period, cases of child abduction for slavery were apparently quite rare. Dandamayev writes:

> "The abduction of children for the purpose of subsequently enslaving them is not, as far as I know, attested at all for the Neo-Babylonian period. At this time, in contrast to the earlier periods, the sale of young children by their parents became a very rare phenomenon."[81]

In any case, kidnapping and slavery are distinct practices, and the illegality of the former does not negate the legality of the other.

Issues seen above, like child slavery and the illegality of kidnapping, lead us to consider the matter of "voluntary/involuntary" distinctions in the practice of slavery; the issue is perhaps more complicated than it first appears. From several examples in both the Old Testament and other ancient Near East texts, it appears that children

---

[81] Dandamayev 1984: 104. He discusses this at greater length on pages 170ff, where he cites examples.

were often seized by creditors and forced into slavery. In II
Kings 4:1 we see, "The wife of a man from the company of the
prophets cried out to Elisha, 'Your servant my husband is
dead, and you know that he revered the Lord. But now his
creditor is coming to take my two boys as his slaves.'" There
was nothing illegal about this action on the part of the
creditor; taking the children as slaves was perfectly within
his legal rights. Failure to repay loans often led to slavery,
either for the one who took the loan or for one of his
household. In Jeremiah 34, the prophet rails against the
slave owners in the land, not because they had taken slaves,
but because they had not released them after the six-year
term of service.

> "Then the word of the Lord came to Jeremiah:
> "This is what the Lord, the God of Israel, says:
> I made a covenant with your ancestors when I
> brought them out of Egypt, out of the land of
> slavery. I said, 'Every seventh year each of you
> must free any fellow Hebrews who have sold
> themselves to you. After they have served you
> six years, you must let them go free.' Your
> ancestors, however, did not listen to me or pay
> attention to me. Recently you repented and did

what is right in my sight: Each of you

proclaimed freedom to your own people. You

even made a covenant before me in the house

that bears my Name. But now you have turned

around and profaned my name; each of you has

taken back the male and female slaves you had

set free to go where they wished. You have

forced them to become your slaves again."

(Jer. 34:12-16)

According to the text, even after releasing them, the masters
had a change of heart, and recaptured their slaves. This
demonstrates clearly that, while entering into debt-slavery,
for example, was technically volitional (either by the will of
the borrower or by his permission when a child or wife were
taken into slavery), once enslaved, one did not have the
freedom to simply leave. Similar situations can be seen in
Nehemiah 5 and in the book of Amos.

This form of slavery also appears in many periods in the
ancient Near East. A particularly vivid example comes from
third millennium Mesopotamia, concerning which Wilcke
notes (as cited above):

"One could conclude that slavery of family
members and in the last resort also that of the
head of the household for his or her debts was
something normal. Therefore the exclamation
of a defaulter 'let them take away the area of
the Inana-irrigation-ditch. But let them not
lead away my children!'"[82]

In short, although the kidnapping of a free citizen was illegal
in the Hebrew Bible, it was also illegal in the wider ancient
Near East. And even though debt-slavery was ultimately
volitional from a technical standpoint, both the Old
Testament and texts from the ancient Near East
demonstrate that the seizure of family members (and heads
of households) was not generally desirable, and once
enslaved, the debtor was not free to leave.

---

[82] Wilcke 2007: 57. An edition of the text can be found in Wilcke 1996: 56-
58 (grand document juridique, K).

*Physical Abuse*

Just as misunderstood, in my opinion, are the laws concerning the physical treatment of the enslaved, particularly in passages like Exodus 21:20-21 and 26-27:

> "20. Anyone who beats their male or female slave with a rod must be punished if the slave dies as a direct result. 21. But they are not to be punished if the slave recovers after a day or two, since the slave is their property . . . 26. An owner who hits a male or female slave in the eye and destroys it must let the slave go free to compensate for the eye. 27. And an owner who knocks out the tooth of a male or female slave must let the slave go free to compensate for the tooth."
> (Exod. 21:20-21, 26-27)

It has often been argued that Exodus 21:20-21 and 26-27 should be understood in one of two ways. First, some have argued that these verses indicate that a master may feel free to beat his slave as much as he likes; as long as he does so in a way that he does not destroy an eye, knock out a tooth, or bring about the slave's immediate death, the law has been upheld. This position, in my opinion, is too extreme. While it may be in keeping with the *letter* of the law, I do not think it would align with the *spirit* of the law. On the other hand, many have argued that verses 20-21 and 26-27 are all dealing with the same type of situation: a master beating his slave. If the slave dies (v. 20), then the master is punished. If the slave does not die (v. 21), then verses 26-27 come into play, and the slave is released because he was abused. Neither of these two positions will stand, either in light of the biblical evidence, or that which we see in the wider ancient Near East.

We must not wish away the reality of the treatment of slaves in ancient cultures, including that which was found in Israel. For example, Proverbs 29:19-21 makes it very clear that:

> "Servants cannot be corrected by mere words;
> though they understand, they will not respond.
> Do you see someone who speaks in haste?
> There is more hope for a fool than for them. A
> servant pampered from youth will turn out to
> be insolent."
> (Prov. 29:19-21)

Throughout the Proverbs, the rod is used as a form of discipline for fools and for children; the place where the rod is generally applied for discipline is on the back. Michael Fox writes, "The proverb gives advice for managing a household. Since a slave is deprived of material interests of his own, he must, it was presumed, be beaten into submission, like a brute animal or a fool."[83] Thus, when we see the rod applied in Exodus 21:20-21, it is being used as a form of discipline with respect to the slave. What is likely in question is the *intent of the master*: if he were to beat the slave so that the slave died immediately, it would be clear that the master intended more than mere discipline. However, if time were to pass between the beating and the death, then it would be assumed that other circumstances may have been involved in causing the death of the slave, and the master would not be held responsible.

In his commentary on Exodus, Sarna writes:

> "The underlying issue, as before, is the determination of intent on the part of the assailant at the time the act was committed . .

---

[83] Fox 2009: 843.

*. a rod* Hebrew shevet [was] the customary instrument for discipline. The right of a master to discipline his slave within reason is recognized. But according to rabbinic exegesis, it is restricted to the use of an implement that does not normally have lethal potentiality, and it may not be applied to a part of the body considered to be particularly vulnerable . . . Should the beaten slave linger more than a day before succumbing, certain new and mitigating circumstances arise. The direct, causal relationship between the master's conduct and the slave's death is now in doubt, for there may have been some unknown intermediate cause. The intent of the master appears less likely to have been homicidal and more likely to have been disciplinary. He is given the benefit of the doubt, especially since he is losing his financial investment, the price of the slave."[84]

---

[84] Sarna 1991: 124.

Philo interpreted the passage in essentially the same way in *The Special Laws III*, lines 141ff:

> "And if he alleges that the stripes he inflicted were meant as a deterrent and not with the intention of causing death, he shall not at once depart with a cheerful heart, but will be brought before the court, there to be examined under strict investigators of the truth as to whether he meant to commit homicide or not; and if he is found to have acted with intentional wickedness and with malice aforethought he must die, and his position as master will avail him nothing to escape the sentence. But if the sufferers do not die on the spot under the lash but survive for one or perhaps two days, the situation is different and the master is not to be held guilty of murder. In this case he is provided with a valuable plea, namely that he did not beat them to death at the time nor yet later when he had them in the house, but suffered them to live as long as they could, even though that time was quite a short time. Furthermore he

may argue that no one is so foolish as to try to harm another when he himself will be wronged thereby. And it is true that anyone who kills a slave injures himself far more, as he deprives himself of the service which he receives from him when alive and loses his value as a piece of property, which may be possibly very considerable."[85]

This common interpretation accords well with verses 26-27; since the head would be considered extremely vulnerable to blows from a wooden rod, if a tooth were to be knocked out or an eye to be damaged or destroyed, this would likely indicate that the master had intended more than simply to discipline his slave.

Additionally, there may have been something special about the eye and the tooth in this context. Not only would damage to these parts of the body likely indicate that the intent was to abuse rather than correct or admonish, but it has also been suggested that these parts of the body were critical for a productive life during the period. Their loss may have

---

[85] Colson 1998: 565-566.

justified the release of the slave due to their importance to sustaining life. Hoffner comments:

> "Why were these two injuries considered the
> most serious? Apparently they were considered
> especially serious because without vision in
> both eyes a person loses the depth perception
> needed to perform most life-sustaining
> agricultural activities, and because in an age
> prior to dental prostheses the loss of teeth
> meant the impairment of one's ability to chew
> and digest life-sustaining food."[86]

---

[86] Hoffner 2008:152. See also Propp 2006: 231-232. "In 21:12-14, 18-19, after describing the consequences for murder and battery, the writer then discusses to what extent the law is the same for slaves (vv 20-21). Similarly, in 21:26-27, having just enunciated the principle of talion, he raises the question: are slaves entitled to talionic retribution? The answer is No; instead, they are generously compensated for their injuries. As in Babylon, talion applies only between social equals." Also, *release him for his eye.* This law is intended to curb slave abuse, particularly beating around the head, which may result not just in loss of an eye or a tooth but in death." Finally, "*tooth.* The equivalence of eye and tooth may seem

Whatever the correct interpretation might be, we can say that there were definite restrictions placed upon the master by the law when it came to the treatment of his slave. As we saw above, however, this was certainly not unique to the Old Testament legal system (e.g. Laws of Hammurabi #115-116 and the *Middle Assyrian Palace Decrees* #18).[87] These texts demonstrate that a master or mistress could not simply do whatever they pleased with the slave. There were restrictions for the type of punishments that could be inflicted upon the slave, and when those punishments were allowable. Should the master beat the slave excessively, he would be held responsible for that offense.

## The Goring Ox

We will close out this section on Exodus 21 by discussing the status of a slave in the case of the goring ox. In verses 28-32, the text deals with the matter of an ox that gores a person to

---

surprising. Who would not rather lose a tooth than an eye? Indeed, given the ancient's poor diet and lack of oral hygiene, people of all classes must have been losing teeth all the time. In the interests of curbing abuse, however, a slave's eye and even his tooth are made economically equivalent to his entire value."

[87] Westbrook 2003b: 383; Magdalene, Wunsch, and Wells 2019: 191.

death and the different punishments that should follow. There are two variables that are to be considered in each case: 1) was the ox in the habit of goring people in the past (and the owner knew about it), and 2) what was the status of the person who was killed? Let's take a look at the passage.

"If a bull gores a man or woman to death, the bull is to be stoned to death, and its meat must not be eaten. But the owner of the bull will not be held responsible. If, however, the bull has had the habit of goring and the owner has been warned but has not kept it penned up and it kills a man or woman, the bull is to be stoned and its owner also is to be put to death. However, if payment is demanded, the owner may redeem his life by the payment of whatever is demanded. This law also applies if the bull gores a son or daughter. If the bull gores a male or female slave, the owner must pay thirty shekels of silver to the master of the slave, and the bull is to be stoned to death (Exod. 21:28-32)."

The logic of the law is relatively straightforward: an ox gores someone to death. If the owner knew that the ox had done this type of thing in the past and did not take appropriate steps to keep the ox penned up, then the owner would be killed along with the ox. If the owner did not know, or the ox had not done this sort of thing before, then the owner would not be held liable; he would be innocent. The remainder of the passage deals with a situation in which the owner *did* know about the ox's habit of goring and did not keep it penned up. The text deals with six types of victims: a man, a woman, a son, a daughter, a male slave, and a female slave. With the first four victims, the owner is to be killed. However, it was possible for the owner to pay to have his life spared, but the sum that was imposed upon him was not fixed.

In v. 32, however, in the case of a male or female slave, the price is set at 30 shekels of silver, likely the going rate of a slave. This sum was to be paid to the slave's owner. Thus, there is a distinction that is made in the law between the value of a free man or members of his family, and that of a slave. Gene Haas writes: "If one's ox gores a slave to death, one is required to pay the slave's master an amount of money, likely the value of the slave (Exod. 21:32). In contrast, if one's ox gores a free Hebrew to death, the penalty is death (Exod. 21:28-31)."[88] Gurtner agrees, "The goring of a slave (v. 32) – male or female – is treated in terms of property loss . . . Recompence for the loss of property is set at thirty didrachmas . . . of silver payable to the master."[89] Propp summarizes the latter portion of Exodus 21 nicely:

> "A bondsman is here regarded as a chattel, not
> as a full human. The case is intermediate
> between one bull killing another and a bull
> killing a freeman. Notably, when a slave is
> murdered by a master, the slain is probably
> accounted a full human (cf. NOTE to 21:20, 'he
> must be avenged, avenged'); when a slave is
> killed by an animal, the slain is property (Paul
> 1970: 83). The only reason for the distinction I
> can see is that the law in 21:20-21 can
> potentially deter masters from slave abuse,
> whereas bulls will always be bulls."[90]

---

[88] Haas 2003: 780.

[89] Gurtner 2013: 392.

[90] Propp 2006: 236.

In short, in the case of the goring ox, the law distinguishes between the penalty for killing a free person and for killing a slave. In the former, the owner's penalty is death (out of which he can pay his way); however, in the latter, the death of the slave falls under property law, and the owner of the ox must make restitution to the owner of the slave by paying him sufficient money to purchase a new slave.

*Summary of Exodus 21*

As we conclude this section of the chapter, let's briefly review what we have determined about slavery from Exodus 21. This portion of Exodus – part of the so-called Covenant Code – is likely the earliest of the three major legal sections that deal with slavery found in the Pentateuch (Exod. 21, Deut. 15, and Lev. 25). We investigated the somewhat elusive term *ḥabiru* and its possible connection to the debt-slaves found in Exodus 21. We determined that, even if there is an etymological connection between *ḥabiru* and the Hebrew word *'ivri* in the Hebrew Bible (and in particular the Pentateuch), the term is used in Exodus 21 as a gentilic, referring to the Hebrews in a way that *contrasts* them with foreigners and other ethnic groups.

We examined the "purchasing" language found in Exodus 21:2, and discovered that we need not soften or alter the meaning of the words "buy" or "purchase" when applying it to slaves; slaves were treated as property, being bought and sold as commodities. We looked at the release of the male slave after six years of service and the situations in which he could find himself, including having to choose between gaining his freedom and staying with his family. By contrast, the female slave was not to be freed after six years, most likely because she was being sold as a concubine or wife to her master. We examined the law of kidnapping in Exodus 21:16, comparing it to other ancient Near Eastern laws, discovering that there is great similarity between the Hebrew Bible and the wider ancient Near Eastern laws.

We then examined the oft-debated passage concerning the beating of slaves in Exodus 21:20-21, as well as verses 26-27, noting several things. First, the text was not intended to give laws that promoted the merciless beating of a slave. Against this, the evidence seems to suggest that the laws were in place to prevent the master from abusing his slave. This does not, however, indicate that masters were not permitted (or even encouraged) to physically discipline their slaves with wooden rods, as this can be seen in both the passage in

111

Exodus as well as in the Proverbs. Finally, in the case of the "goring ox," we examined the distinctions that were made between free persons and slaves, noting that slaves were not considered to be of equal value to free persons.

## Deuteronomy 15

The passage in Deuteronomy 15 parallels concepts dealt with in Exodus 21, particularly with respect to the release of Hebrew debt-slaves. However, some of the laws in this passage appear to have changed or developed when compared to Exodus 21. In this section, we will examine the likely developments, beginning with Deuteronomy 15:12-18:

> "If any of your people—Hebrew men or women—sell themselves to you and serve you six years, in the seventh year you must let them go free. And when you release them, do not send them away empty-handed. Supply them liberally from your flock, your threshing floor and your winepress. Give to them as the Lord your God has blessed you. Remember that you were slaves in Egypt and the Lord your God redeemed you. That is why I give you this command today. But if your servant says

to you, "I do not want to leave you," because he loves you and your family and is well off with you, then take an awl and push it through his earlobe into the door, and he will become your servant for life. Do the same for your female servant. Do not consider it a hardship to set your servant free, because their service to you these six years has been worth twice as much as that of a hired hand. And the Lord your God will bless you in everything you do."
(Deut. 15:12-18)

There are two apparent developments seen in this passage that require attention. The first is the (possible) addition of the six-year-release provision for the female slave. The second is the regulation for sending the released slave out with significant provisions in order to establish him/herself after their term of servitude. We will deal with each of these developments in turn.

*Female Slave Release*

One of the things that we noticed in Exodus 21 was the distinction that was made between the release of Israelite male and female slaves. Male slaves were to "go out" after serving six years, while female slaves were not to be released. Now, however, when we read Deuteronomy 15:17, we see that the seventh-year release is also to be applied to the female slave. Is this a genuine development in the law from the earlier Covenant Code of Exodus 21, or is the situation distinct here in Deuteronomy 15, concerning a different type of female slave?

To state the problem succinctly, there appears to be a contradiction between Exodus 21 and Deuteronomy 15, particularly with respect to the release of the female slave in the seventh year. There are at least two possible explanations for this inconsistency. The first would be that there was a development in the laws over time, in which the female slave was granted the same release as the male slave in Exodus 21. We see these types of changes taking place when we examine Leviticus 25 (see later in this chapter); there the passage almost certainly acts to rework Exodus 21 with respect to, for example, the taking of Hebrew slaves. This may indicate that the writer in Deuteronomy 15 – as was done in Leviticus 25 – added the stipulation that the female slave was also to be released in response to Exodus 21. Commenting on the changes seen in Leviticus 25, Milgrom argues:

"I submit that one has to consider seriously the possibility that Leviticus deliberately omits any mention of the Israelite's wife in order to make a legal statement: she does not leave the creditor's service because she does not enter it. Here, Leviticus is conducting a tacit polemic against Exod. 21:7-11 (and Deut. 15:12, 17): the wife may not be indentured!"[91]

It seems that, in Milgrom's opinion, both Exodus 21 and Deuteronomy 15 speak to essentially the same situation, the latter passage developing the former.

Another possibility is that a different scenario is envisioned in Deuteronomy 15; the female slave who is to be released in the same way as the male slave had not been taken into slavery in the capacity of a concubine or wife. As a "standard" type of Hebrew slave, she would be entitled to release after six years. Frymer-Kenski notes:

"According to the Book of the Covenant, if a man sells his daughter as an 'amah, she goes

---

[91] Milgrom 2001: 2224.

out if the master, acquiring another wife, does not provide her with her wifely allotment. But she does not go out as slaves do, after six years (Exod. 21:7). Deuteronomy calls for the parallel release of male or female Hebrew slaves (Deut. 15:12). The difference may be the disappearance of sale-marriage, in which the *'amah* would want a permanent arrangement."[92]

In short, it is possible that the release of the female slave in Deuteronomy 15 is akin to the development seen in Leviticus 25, which arguably turns Exodus 21 on its head in several ways (e.g., no Hebrew "slaves," wives cannot be indentured, etc.; see arguments below by Milgrom and Levinson). Thus, Deuteronomy 15 and Exodus 21 both speak of the same type of female slave, with Deuteronomy now calling for the parallel release of both male and female slaves. However, it may also be that Deuteronomy 15 is speaking only about a general female slave, and not one that has specifically been sold as a concubine or wife, as in Exodus 21. As we will

---

[92] Frymer-Kenski 2003: 1006.

discuss later in more detail, it may also be that Leviticus simply considers the situation of a *paterfamilias* who has already sold his (wife and) children into debt-slavery, and eventually he must follow (or they all go together at once). At the Jubilee, in this situation, all would be released together. Thus, there may be no contradiction between the individual passages in this respect.

*Release with Provisions*

Perhaps the most obvious development that appears in Deuteronomy 15 – when compared to the Covenant Code of Exodus 21 – is the requirement for the master to release his slave after six years *with significant provisions in hand.* "And when you release them, do not send them away empty-handed. Supply them liberally from your flock, your threshing floor and your winepress. Give to them as the Lord your God has blessed you" (Deut. 15:13-14).

The rationale for providing the newly released slave with substantive means can be seen in the overall context of the passage. In vv. 1-6, the text stipulates that all debts owed by Israelites were to be cancelled every seven years. This was to aid in keeping poverty at a minimum – as much as possible – for the nation of Israel. Similarly, in vv. 7-11, if fellow

Israelites were to fall on hard times and desperately needed loans, their brethren were not to calculate how close they were to the year of cancelling debts. Instead, they were to provide for their countrymen as the Lord had provided for them.

Thus, when we come to the release of slaves in Deuteronomy 15:12-18, the generosity that the master was to show to his Hebrew slave was to be in the same vein. Ostensibly, this was to keep the slave – at least to some extent – from falling back into poverty after their release. Having served the master for six years, it would have been difficult for the slave to go out on their own having no financial wherewithal. This development in the law provided the slave with the ability to make a fresh start. As Christensen writes, "The reason the servant was not to be sent 'away empty-handed' was to make sure that the person did not have to borrow for basic sustenance."[93]

---

[93] Christensen 2001: 320.

Nelson summarizes this section nicely:

> "This law represents a radical rewriting of the
> manumission law in the Covenant Code (Exod.
> 21:2-6). The differences are telling. Although
> Deuteronomy retains the main case of
> manumission and the subcase regarding one
> who wishes to stay, it adds an entirely new
> requirement to provide a grubstake for the
> released slave. Exodus operates from the point
> of view of the buyer and owner. Deuteronomy
> emphasizes the desperate perspective of the
> enslaved kindred. Deuteronomy shifts from the
> predominantly third-person reference to the
> slave found in Exodus and directs the
> responsibility straight at the 'you' of the
> slaveowning audience."[94]

---

[94] Nelson 2002: 197.

Chapter Three

## Deuteronomy 20

While not a "slave passage," strictly speaking, I would like to briefly discuss Deuteronomy 20, which concerns the procedures set in place for going to war against other nations, including those dwelling inside and outside of the promised land. While this may seem like an odd chapter to examine in a discussion about slavery, it has been used to argue against the existence of chattel slavery, particularly in Leviticus 25. Specifically, it is sometimes suggested that the foreigners who were allowed to be taken by the Israelites according to Leviticus 25:44-46 were strictly *prisoners of war*; this conclusion is then linked to Deuteronomy 20, where war-time practices are discussed. Thus, it seems prudent for us to consider this section of Deuteronomy with an eye toward the taking of prisoners and any possible connection it might have to the laws concerning slavery.

Deuteronomy 20 is broken up into three sections: preparations for going to war (vv. 1-9), rules for engaging distant cities (vv. 10-15), and rules for people groups inside the land of Israel (vv. 16-20). Briefly stated, there were different warfare regulations applied to cities located *outside* of the land of Israel than those applied to those found *inside* the land. For those cities at a distance, the Israelites were to approach with terms of peaceful surrender. Tigay writes:

> "Offer it *shalom*, here meaning terms of
> surrender, a promise to spare the city and its
> inhabitants if they agree to serve you. The
> same idiom appears in an Akkadian letter
> from Mari: 'when he had besieged that city, he
> offered it terms of submission [*salimam*].'"[95]

If the city were to accept these terms of surrender, no harm was to come to them; they would become the servants of the Israelites, subject to forced labor (Hebrew מַס *mas*). Again, Tigay writes, "Hebrew *mas* refers to a contingent of forced laborers working for the state. They were employed in agriculture and public works, such as construction."[96]

While this type of subjugation might seem oppressive, this scenario was actually to be preferred to its alternative. If that city were to refuse the terms of surrender, then the nation of Israel was to besiege it, and when it fell, they were

---

[95] Tigay 1996: 188.
[96] Ibid., 189.

to kill all of the men, and take the women, children, and livestock as plunder. As Woods correctly notes, "This is not the practice of being 'put under the ban' (*herem*) that relates to the cities of the land itself, but rather an emasculation to ensure no further threat."[97] In other words, by putting to death all of the men of the city, there would be little to no chance of that city posing any additional threat to the nation of Israel, as all of their fighting forces would have been destroyed.

When this passage is used to construct an argument against the use of chattel slavery, I often hear it presented in this way:

> The foreign slaves that are mentioned in the biblical laws (especially in Lev. 25:44-46) are actually prisoners of war. What else would the Israelites have done with these POWs? There were only three options: 1) let them live and remain in their cities, 2) kill them, or 3) make them slaves. Now, the first was not a realistic option, as it would have allowed Israel's

[97] Woods 2011: 231.

enemies to regroup and attack them again. The second option was often employed, but was not as merciful as the third option, which would be to enslave the people and bring them to Israel, where foreigners were to be treated well. Thus, while the foreigners were sometimes enslaved, these were POWs, and their enslavement was actually an act of mercy. This should not, therefore, be considered typical 'chattel slavery.'

As we have just seen, the biblical laws in Deuteronomy set forth regulations for going to war against Israel's enemies. If a foreign city were to surrender, they were simply made to serve as forced labor. However, if they did not surrender, the men were to be killed and the women, children, and livestock were to be taken as plunder. Let's pause for a second. If the city did not surrender, then the Israelites were to lay siege to it and, when it falls, they were to kill all the men. Again… they were to kill *all the men*. This emasculation of the city rendered it essentially defenseless, as there would no longer be fighting forces within it. Only the women, children, and livestock would remain, and would be taken as plunder.

This leads to the question, "Did Deuteronomy 20 anticipate prisoners of war?" The answer would seem to be in the negative (as far as the text is concerned), as those taken into captivity were not combatants; they are more appropriately to be considered plunder or the spoils of war. The idea that there were bands of soldiers that would be left behind who must either be guarded or enslaved does not appear to be found in the text, and is simply not in keeping with the rules of engagement set forth in Deuteronomy 20. The men, who made up the fighting forces, were either to be forced to serve as *corvée* labor (having accepted the terms of peace and surrender), or were to be killed, thereby emasculating the city.

It is worth noting that this stipulation in the law (offering peace or emasculating the city and taking the rest as plunder) only applied to a certain type of city:

> "This is how you are to treat all the cities that are at a distance from you and do not belong to the nations nearby. However, in the cities of the nations the Lord your God is giving you as an inheritance, do not leave alive anything

that breathes".

(Deut. 20:15)

This command to offer peace initially and engage in war if that peace is rejected only applied to the nations that were outside of the land of Israel; those inside of the land were not afforded these options. They were to be annihilated, as they had been placed under the "ban."

In short, the idea that the procedures in Deuteronomy 20 would result in fighting men that would be left over during war time, and that these fighting forces became the slaves that are pictured in Leviticus 25:44-46 is simply not something that the law accounted for. According to the text, the soldiers were to be killed. Period. It seems, therefore, that the foreigners who were pictured in Leviticus 25:44-46 were not the prisoners of war left over from the battles described in Deuteronomy 20.

Leviticus 25

Perhaps no other chapter concerning slavery in the Hebrew Bible is as cited or debated as Leviticus 25, particularly verses 44-46.

"Your male and female slaves are to come from
the nations around you; from them you may
buy slaves. You may also buy some of the
temporary residents living among you and
members of their clans born in your country,
and they will become your property. You can
bequeath them to your children as inherited
property and can make them slaves for life, but
you must not rule over your fellow Israelites
ruthlessly".

(Lev. 25:44-46)

What makes this passage so contentious becomes
immediately apparent to the reader: the Israelites were
allowed to purchase foreign slaves, who were able to be kept
for life and passed down as inherited property. Given the
highly contentious nature of these verses, and although it
might seem be a bit unorthodox, I would like to quote a
number of ancient Near Eastern and biblical scholars before
we analyze the text itself, in order to demonstrate what the
current scholarly consensus is on this passage. To be clear,
these few citations from both so-called "conservative" and
"liberal" scholars are in no way intended to suggest that my
position is correct simply because these scholars agree with

me. However, because one of the expressed aims of this book is to provide the reader with citations and arguments that represent the positions of the mainstream scholarly community, I think that a grouping of citations at this juncture is appropriate.

Bernard Levinson:

> "Section 2 of the law sanctions what section 1 prohibits – holding slaves as chattel – but restricts such slaveholding to non-Israelite slaves taken 'from the nations round you' (v. 44b) . . . Figure 3 below demonstrates the textual reworking that permits Leviticus 25 to restrict the purchase, ownership, and inheritance of slaves to the category of foreigners."[98]

---

[98] Levinson 2005: 620.

Gregory Chirichigno:

> "The reference to foreign slaves in Lev. 25.44-45 indicates clearly that these slaves were the permanent property of their owners."[99]

Gene Haas:

> "A second characteristic of ancient Near Eastern slavery reflected in the Pentateuch is that a slave does not have the rights of a free person; he or she is 'the owner's property' (Ex. 21:21). As such, slaves may be left to one's children as inheritance (Lev 25:46)."[100]

Tikva Frymer-Kenski:

> "Foreign slaves bought from the surrounding nations or from foreigners living in Israel do not go out: they are inherited as property (Lev. 25:44-46)."[101]

---

[99] Chirichigno 1993: 147.

[100] Haas 2003: 779.

[101] Frymer-Kenski 2003: 1006.

Jan Joosten:

> "According to 25:44ff, Israelite slaves must go
> free at the jubilee, but the sons of the
> sojourners . . . may be enslaved for life."[102]

Kenneth Kitchen:

> "*Foreign Slaves*. 1. Unlike Hebrew slaves,
> these could be enslaved permanently and
> handed on with other family property (Lv. xxv.
> 44-46)"(original emphasis).[103]

Jay Sklar:

> "The text addresses two natural questions that
> arise at this point for the Israelites (vv. 44-
> 46a). First, may they have 'permanent
> servants'? Yes, but permanent servants must
> come from *the nations* surrounding Israel (v.
> 44) or 'from' foreign nationals living as
> *temporary residents* in their midst (v. 45; 'from'
> is better than NIV's *some of*). Second, do these

---

[102] Joosten 1996: 64.

[103] Kitchen 1962: 1196.

also go free automatically in the Jubilee? No, these servants may serve *for life* (v. 46), although this law does not require that."[104]

R. K. Harrison:

"Having once been redeemed from slavery, the Hebrews can never again be sold as slaves (42). Such is not the case with non-Israelites, however, who can be both bought and sold in that way, and even bequeathed to one's successors (46)."[105]

Daisy Yulin-Tsai:

"An Israelite slave should never be treated as property per se, but only as belonging to YHWH. As a result, Lev. 25:44-46a clarifies that if one wants to possess permanent slaves as their *inherited property* that may be bequeathed to his children, he can acquire aliens or the sojourners among Israel . . . If an

---

[104] Sklar 2014: 306.
[105] Harrison 1980: 228.

Israelite wants to obtain a permanent slave as an *inheritable property* for their children, he can *only* buy it among the non-Israelite!"[106]

Muhammad Dandamayev:

"In later periods of Israelite society, the influx of prisoners of war was very limited, and for this reason the basic source of slaves was natural reproduction. The next source of slavery was obtaining slaves through purchase from neighboring nations. This source was in every possible way encouraged by biblical instructions (Lev. 25:44-46, etc.; cf. also Eccl. 2:7). Such slaves were legally considered the absolute property of their owners, and their status was permanent: they were sold, passed on by way of inheritance, pawned, and branded or marked like livestock."[107]

---

[106] Tsai 2014: 107.

[107] Dandamayev 1992: 66.

Jacob Milgrom:

> "The assumption here is that the alien is a
> chattel-slave, not a debt-slave . . . This law
> merely indicates that the jubilee does not
> apply to non-Israelite slaves."[108]

Bernard Jackson:

> "The distinction between temporary debt-
> slaves and permanent foreign slaves (who may
> be bequeathed 'to your sons after you, to
> inherit as a possession for ever') is made
> explicit in a later biblical source, *Lev.* 25:39-46
> (which rejects even the use of the term *eved* for
> the Hebrew debt-slave)."[109]

Harry Hoffner:

> "The 'Hebrew slave' laws occupy a special place
> in the Book of the Covenant. That such slaves
> served only for a set period demonstrates that
> they were in fact indentured servants or debt

---

[108] Milgrom 2001: 2230.
[109] Jackson 2006: 82.

slaves. Such slaves enjoyed a privilege not accorded to slaves from foreign sources: they could only be lifelong slaves by voluntarily renouncing their emancipation rights."[110]

Kristine Garroway

"According to Lev. 25:44-45, the Israelites are given permission to purchase and permanently enslave the children of the 'foreigners,' גוי and גרים surrounding Israel. By extension, this means that if an Israelite owns a foreign slave, any children the slave produces are bound to their master's house."[111]

One of the key aspects of this passage – as seen in the quotes cited above – is the distinction that is made between Hebrew slaves and foreign slaves. The regulations found in vv. 44-46 stand in contrast to the laws that have come before concerning the treatment of an Israelite who has fallen into poverty. There are different levels of poverty into which an Israelite can fall in the chapter; for example, in v. 25 we read,

---

[110] Hoffner 2008: 148.
[111] Garroway 2014: 137.

"If one of your fellow Israelites becomes poor and sells some of their property, their nearest relative is to come and redeem what they have sold." In addition, in v. 35, "If any of your fellow Israelites becomes poor and are unable to support themselves among you, help them as you would a foreigner and stranger, so they can continue to live among you."

In the first scenario, the Israelite has become poor enough to necessitate the sale of his property in order to survive. In this case, a near relative is to redeem the land that has been sold. In the second scenario, if an Israelite becomes so poor that they are unable to support themselves, the community is to come to their aid. However, there is a third scenario with which the text deals; in v. 39, "If any of your fellow Israelites become poor and sell themselves to you, do not make them work as slaves. They are to be treated as hired workers or temporary residents among you; they are to work for you until the Year of Jubilee." In short:

- If an Israelite sells their land → it gets redeemed.
- If an Israelite can't support themselves → the community aids them.
- If an Israelite sells themselves into slavery → don't treat them like a slave, but like a hired worker.

This is how the Israelites were to care for their brethren. Blenkinsopp summarizes:

> "The same solicitude for the poor fellow Israelite is expressed in the Holiness Code, which requires support of the poor, as an obligation not as charity, and states explicitly that the insolvent 'brother' who sells himself must not be treated as a slave (Lev. 25:35-39)."[112]

As we noted above concerning the laws in Deuteronomy 15, there also appears to be a development in the laws of Leviticus 25 when compared to both Exodus 21 and Deuteronomy 15. Bernard Levinson, in a 2005 article in the *Journal of Biblical Literature*, argued that Leviticus 25 was written to essentially turn Exodus 21 "on its head" with respect to its laws about slavery. If you remember, Exodus 21 says that you *can* have Hebrew slaves, but you must release them after six years of service. However, here in Leviticus 25, we see that the Israelites were NOT to treat their brethren as slaves, but rather as "hired workers." So, given this

---

[112] Blenkinsopp 1988: 258.

development and restriction on holding fellow Israelites as slaves, the question would naturally arise: "If an Israelite cannot have another Israelite as a slave, whom *can* he have as a slave?"

The answer comes in v. 44: "Your male and female slaves are to come from the nations around you; from them you may buy slaves." In other words, while Leviticus 25 is creating a better situation for the *Israelites* who fall into poverty, *this improvement does not apply to the foreigner*. Thus, if an Israelite wants to own slaves, he can no longer obtain them from among his brethren; slaves could only be acquired from among the foreigners, either from the nations around them, or from the foreign residents that were living among them. Sklar notes:

> "The text addresses two natural questions that arise at this point for the Israelites (vv. 44-46a). First, may they have 'permanent servants'? Yes, but permanent servants must come from *the nations* surrounding Israel (v. 44) or 'from' foreign nationals living as *temporary residents* in their midst . . . Second, do these also go free automatically in the

Jubilee? No, these servants may serve *for life* (v. 46), although this law does not require that."[113]

Additionally, as cited above, Levinson writes:

"Section 2 of the law sanctions what section 1 prohibits – holding slaves as chattel – but restricts such slaveholding to non-Israelite slaves taken 'from the nations round you' (v. 44b) . . . [this] demonstrates the textual reworking that permits Leviticus 25 to restrict the purchase, ownership, and inheritance of slaves to the category of foreigners."[114]

---

[113] Sklar 2014: 306. Note that, although Sklar clearly understands the passage to speak of permanent slavery that is distinguished from that which can be enforced upon fellow Israelites, he maintains a standard apologetic position with respect to the slavery that was advocated in the law. The same is true of Baker 2015: 14. "Only one law permits chattel slavery (Lev. 25:44-46a), and even this does not encourage it, but limits it to those outside the covenant *community*: residents of other countries and foreign residents in Israel."

[114] Levinson 2005: 620.

Daisy Yulin Tsai (also cited above) concurs:

> "An Israelite slave should never be treated as
> property per se, but only as belonging to
> YHWH. As a result, Lev. 25:44-46a clarifies
> that if one wants to possess permanent slaves
> as their *inherited property* that may be
> bequeathed to his children, he can acquire
> aliens or the sojourners among Israel," and "If
> an Israelite wants to obtain a permanent slave
> as an *inheritable property* for their children, he
> can only buy it among the non-Israelite!"[115]

In short, if an Israelite wanted to own a slave, Leviticus 25
restricted him to only purchasing foreigners; he could no
longer treat Israelites as slaves.

Now that we understand the general layout of the chapter,
let's get into some of the details. There are several things
from the Hebrew of the text that are worth noting in this
discussion. First, v. 45 mentions the "temporary resident" –
who are these people? The Hebrew word used here is

---

[115] Tsai 2014: 107.

*toshavim*, the plural of the noun translated "temporary resident" (תּוֹשָׁב *toshav*); however, the definition of the word *toshav* has been the subject of some debate. In 2014, Joram Mayshar at Hebrew University, Jerusalem, wrote an article entitled, "Who was the Toshav?".[116] The article concluded that the term referred to a "tenant farmer," one who works land that does not belong to him; instead, he pays rent to the owner of the field, keeping the surplus for himself. Whether Mayshar is correct in his identification is not critical to this discussion; the important point to note is that identifying the specific nature of the *toshav* is not entirely straightforward.

Generally speaking, terms for foreigners in the Hebrew Bible tend to take nuanced meanings in different passages, depending on the context. In fact, in 2011, an entire edited volume was dedicated to this topic, entitled *The Foreigner and the Law: Perspectives from the Hebrew Bible and the Ancient Near East*. In spite of these complexities and nuanced meanings, what we *can* say is that these "resident

---

[116] Mayshar 2014.

aliens" were certainly not Israelites, but foreigners who were residing in the land on a long-term basis.[117]

This identification is important for another reason; some – usually (if not always) on social media – have argued that the law allowing Israelites to keep foreign slaves for life was actually meant to be *beneficial* to the foreign slave. It is suggested that these foreigners would have had no land and no ability to fend for themselves; being a slave would have actually been *preferable* to being free. Some have gone so far as to say that the foreigners may have *sought out* slavery in Israel, coming from their foreign nations to be enslaved by the Israelites.

The idea that the foreigners from the nations around Israel, as well as the alien residents or tenant farmers living in the land would have had no land to return to after their release is simply inaccurate. The reality is that slaves in the ancient world were extraordinarily common, and biblical law allowed the Israelites to purchase slaves from these foreign nations,

---

[117] The context also makes it clear that there is a sharp contrast between those that can be taken as genuine slaves (foreigners) and those that cannot (Israelites). See Milgrom 2001: 2229-30 for a detailed argument.

who were often debt-slaves that had fallen into the hands of their foreign creditors, who then had the right to sell them. It is also quite likely that the foreign tenant farmers living in the land of Israel had taken out loans and subsequently fallen into debt-slavery; these, as opposed to the Israelites, could be kept indefinitely; there was no law requiring their release.

Furthermore, the idea that the foreigner would want to come to Israel to serve as a permanent slave, or would want to leave their free resident alien status to become a slave, is not only absent from the text, but goes against the very nature of the laws themselves. The entire point of Leviticus 25 is to emphasize that making someone a slave (*'eved*) and keeping them indefinitely is an *undesirable situation*; the Israelites were no longer allowed to treat their fellow Israelites in this manner. The text says, essentially, that they cannot treat their own people in this way; if they wanted slaves, they could only get them from the people who were not their brethren. Slavery was not a sought-after position, and the laws of release built into the legal system were in *support* of the enslaved, as we would expect.

Thus, when we examine the context of Leviticus 25:44-46, we see several things. First, chapter 25 focuses on the year of Jubilee, and the release of property and individuals after a set period of time. In this context, the text describes an Israelite who falls into poverty, and how other Israelites are to treat and support him. If the destitute Israelite must sell himself to another, his master must not treat him as an 'eved, but instead as a hired worker. If an Israelite wanted to purchase a slave, therefore, he must do so from among the nations around or the foreign residents who were living in the land. These foreigners could be treated as slaves, kept as permanent property, and passed on to their children as inheritance. As we have discussed, this did not mean that, because they were property, the master had *carte blanche* to treat them in any manner that he liked.

*Property*

Before we leave Leviticus 25:44-46, we should discuss some of the Hebrew terms that are used in these verses. Let's begin with the word "property," (אֲחֻזָּה *'ahuzzah*). In various discussions and presentations on social media, many have argued that this term does not indicate that the person is actually owned, but simply refers to the *labor output* of an individual. If correct, this interpretation would soften the tone of the passage, leaving the master merely owning the work or labor of the slave, rather than their personhood. As we saw above, slaves were commonly bought and sold, just as they are in this passage. Does this purchasing, therefore, simply refer to the buying and/or selling of labor output?

The word *'ahuzzah* appears many times in Leviticus 25, almost exclusively referring to the portions of land that were allotted to the Israelites. It is also used in passages like Genesis 47:11, where Joseph gives his family an *'ahuzzah* in Egypt: "So Joseph settled his father and his brothers in Egypt and gave them property in the best part of the land, the district of Rameses, as Pharaoh directed." The noun *'ahuzzah* can also be joined with other words to specify the type of property that is being spoken of, as in Genesis 23:20: "So the field and the cave in it were deeded to Abraham by the Hittites as a burial site (*'ahuzzah* + *qever* "grave")." While the word is normally used to refer to *land* or *objects* that are owned, it is striking that the word *'ahuzzah* is used in Leviticus 25:45-46 to refer to *purchased slaves*. Indeed, Milgrom notes, "This is the one place where this term is applied to persons. Canaanite slaves, like Israel's land, are permanent possessions."[118] Thus, in the same way that objects can be considered "property," so also can slaves. Levine observes, "In ancient law, slaves were often regarded as having a legal status parallel to that of land. Just as the land was a 'holding' (*'aḥuzzah*) to be handed down within families, so were slaves."[119]

Nevertheless, some have turned to the following verses in this passage in order to demonstrate that the term "property" should only be equated with labor output. Leviticus 25:47-53 read:

> "If a foreigner residing among you becomes rich and any of your fellow Israelites become poor and sell themselves to the foreigner or to a member of the foreigner's clan, they retain the right of redemption after they have sold themselves. One of their relatives may redeem them: An uncle or a cousin or any blood relative in their clan may redeem them. Or if they prosper, they may redeem themselves.

---

[118] Milgrom 2001: 2230.
[119] Levine 1989: 180.

They and their buyer are to count the time

from the year they sold themselves up to the

Year of Jubilee. The price for their release is to

be based on the rate paid to a hired worker for

that number of years. If many years remain,

they must pay for their redemption a larger

share of the price paid for them. If only a few

years remain until the Year of Jubilee, they

are to compute that and pay for their

redemption accordingly. They are to be treated

as workers hired from year to year; you must

see to it that those to whom they owe service

do not rule over them ruthlessly."

(Lev. 25:47-53)

The situation presented in this passage involves an Israelite

that sells himself to a foreign resident. At the time of their

redemption – either by a kinsman or by himself, using his

own accumulated wealth – he should determine the correct

redemption price by calculating the length of time that he

would have served until the Jubilee. What is significant here,

however, is that the text is describing how an *Israelite* is to

be viewed and treated, *not a foreigner*. Not only is the word

*'ahuzzah* not used in this section to refer to the Hebrew slave,

it is, in fact, not mentioned at all. Remember, the contrast in this passage is between how an *Israelite* who sells himself into slavery is to be treated compared to how a *foreigner* may be treated. One of the central points is that the Israelite cannot be treated as a slave and must be released at the Jubilee. The foreigner, on the other hand, need not be released, and may be treated as a slave.

*Rigor*

Finally, I would like to briefly mention the word "rigor," which appears several times in Leviticus 25. There has been some debate as to both the meaning of the word itself, as well as what it refers to in this particular passage. The Hebrew word translated "rigor"(פֶּרֶךְ *pereḥ*), is defined as "violence, slavery; always with בְּ, meaning violent (Ex 1:13f; Lev 25:43, 46, 53; Ezek 34:4)."[120] The Greek word used to translate *pereḥ* here is μόχθος *mokthos*, which is defined by Muraoka as *"physical hardship, hard work, . . . labor, exertion, hardship"*[121] When we view the passages in which this term appears in similar contexts, we find that the Israelites were

---

[120] Koehler and Baumgartner 1996: #7735, *s.v.* פֶּרֶךְ.

[121] Muraoka 2009: 469a, s.v. μόχθος (emphasis in text).

treated with "rigor" in Egypt (Exod. 1:13), as well as in the later period, during the time of the prophets (Ezek. 34:4).

Thus, it would appear that the use of the term *pereḥ* in these contexts describes the general way in which the slave is treated. This type of treatment, however, can appear to be at odds with other passages in the Hebrew Bible, which describe how foreigners are to be treated. Milgrom writes, "Implied is that the alien slave may be treated harshly, but according to Job 31:13, 15, such treatment is not acceptable to YHWH."[122] Without going into detail concerning the difficulties of this section of Leviticus, there are certain developments and changes that appear in the text that appear to be at odds with other parts of the biblical text (similar to those discussed above with respect to Exod. 21 and Deut. 15). Gerstenberger hypothesizes that v. 46b might contain an answer to an earlier contradiction:

> "How can a contradiction this obvious be
> explained? Is this a concession to large
> property owners who own slaves, owners who
> on the basis of vv. 35-38 must take financial

---

[122] Milgrom 2001: 2232.

losses? The explicit distinction between foreign slaves and the impoverished natives in the present wording of v. 46b ('but as for your fellow Israelites, no one shall rule over the other with hardness') might allude to this."[123]

Whatever the case may be, there is an implied contrast between the Hebrew and foreign slave with respect to the term "rigor," which appears to allow for the foreign slave to be treated as a genuine *'eved*, something that is explicitly condemned for the Israelite in the passage.

## Conclusion

While this chapter is in no way intended to exhaustively deal with all aspects of slavery in these passages (much less all exegetical and interpretive cruxes), I have sought to identify some of the more essential or debated issues, while presenting both the interpretive difficulties and their likely or proposed solutions. In Exodus 21, the so-called "Covenant Code," we discussed the identity of the "Hebrew" slaves,

---

[123] Gerstenberger 1996: 390.

determining that they were not foreign slaves connected to the *ḥabiru* of the wider ancient Near East. We examined the laws concerning the release of Hebrew slaves in the passage, including both males and females. We also sought to elucidate the meaning and intent of vv. 20-21 and 26-27 concerning the beating of a slave. Finally, we looked briefly at the significance of the ox-goring passage and what this suggested about the status of slaves.

We then turned to Deuteronomy 15, where we saw a development in the laws concerning the six-year release of a Hebrew slave. Here, the text applies said release to both male and female slaves, and we examined the rationale behind this possible development. In Deuteronomy 20, we discussed the rules of engagement that the Israelites were to practice when going to war, both against those cities inside as well as outside of the land of Israel. Perhaps most significantly, we determined that so-called "prisoners of war" were not part of the law in Deuteronomy 20, as the only survivors taken as plunder would have been women, children, and livestock. This would likely discredit an interpretation that assumes foreigners taken as slaves in passages like Leviticus 25:44-46 are simply POWs taken as a result of the laws in Deuteronomy 20.

Chapter Three

Finally, we looked into the oft-mentioned and disputed passage, Leviticus 25:44-46. The text was examined in order to answer questions such as, "Who were the foreigners? Could they be kept for life? What do the words 'rigor' and 'property' mean in this context? What is the overall point of this passage?" It was determined that there is a strong contrast set forth between an Israelite that sells himself into slavery and a foreigner who is purchased as a slave. The Israelite cannot be kept for life and must not be treated as a slave (but as a hired worker). This was not so for the foreigner, who could be kept as a genuine slave for life and passed on as inheritance.

In conclusion it is the intent of this brief exegetical analysis of the primary legal passages concerning slavery in the Hebrew Bible to provide a firm foundation upon which the reader can build. Sources have been cited liberally, and the mainstream interpretive models have hopefully been adequately presented. In the next chapter, we will examine other common objections to the reality of slavery in the Hebrew Bible that I hear, particularly on social media. I hope to provide substantial and useful responses to these objections whenever possible.

150

# CHAPTER FOUR:

# Other Common Objections to the Reality of Slavery in the Hebrew Bible

Slavery in the Hebrew Bible is one of the many topics that seem to never really fall out of popularity, whether we like it or not. Sometimes these topics remain popular because there is no clear or definitive answer to be found in the text. Other topics, however, seem to resurface for debate over and over again because of their implications. For example, God's command to kill all of the inhabitants of a city or region, or causing the death of David's newborn baby to punish David for his sin: these continue to be debated, not because they are necessarily unclear, but because of what they might imply about God. The same appears to be true for the issue of slavery in the Old Testament.

For example, I would like to quote Gerstenberger's commentary on Leviticus 25:44-46:

"All the more terrifying does the unprotected
condition of foreigners and their descendants
that comes to light in the following sentences
seem to us (vv. 44-46). They are to be at full
disposal for slave labor. These genuine slaves
can be imported from outside, or can fall into
bondage in the land of Israel itself, for
example, through economic insolvency (v. 45).
The laws of the year of release do not apply to
these 'aliens dwelling in the land' and for their
descendants (!). This is shocking when
compared with the basic rule of Leviticus
19:33f."[124]

Gerstenberger's point here is not that Leviticus 19:33-34 is
generally ambiguous ("When a stranger resides with you in
your land, you shall do him no wrong. The stranger who
resides with you shall be to you as a native among you, and
you shall love him as yourself; for you were aliens in the land
of Egypt; I am the Lord your God"). Nor is Leviticus 25:44-46
particularly unclear:

---

[124] Gerstenberger 1996: 390.

"Your male and female slaves are to come from
the nations around you; from them you may
buy slaves. You may also buy some of the
temporary residents living among you and
members of their clans born in your country,
and they will become your property. You can
bequeath them to your children as inherited
property and can make them slaves for life, but
you must not rule over your fellow Israelites
ruthlessly."

(Lev. 25:44-46)

While there may be specific nuances in these verses that
make some of these interpretative cruxes challenging to
resolve, the overall point is clear. And it is this clarity – and
the apparent contradiction that it creates from our modern
point of view – that has resulted in the continued debate in
this passage, and others like it. For example, how can God
say to love the "stranger" or "resident alien," loving him as
yourself, and yet condone the purchase and permanent
ownership (as property) of a sojourner? It would seem that
Leviticus 25:44-46 is so often debated, not because it is
difficult to understand, but because of what it might say
about God.

We have addressed a number of difficulties in the first three chapters of this book; there you can find more detailed analysis of the primary passages related to slavery in the Old Testament, as well as descriptions of the laws and practices concerning slavery in the Hebrew Bible and in the wider ancient Near East. This chapter, however, will address some of the more common responses that I have received to my presentations of slavery in the Old Testament that have not been addressed above. Many of these responses appear to arise from what the texts about slavery imply about other issues (e.g., the nature of morality). It is my hope that, in addressing these objections that have been raised, we can not only gain greater clarity on a topic that is (in my opinion) not as elusive as some might argue, but also allow for the ancient world – with its opinions and practices – to be understood in light of its social and moral contexts, which are often quite different from ours.

## Objection #1

> "Don't verses like Leviticus 19:33-34 and
> Exodus 12:48 demonstrate that foreigners
> were given the same rights as Israelites and
> were to be treated with love and kindness?
> How could God condone or endorse slavery and
> also give these commands? We must be
> misunderstanding passages on slavery like
> Leviticus 25:44-46."

As you might imagine, I hear this objection a lot. As I
mentioned above, it is a legitimate question to ask! While
there are certainly different types of foreigners mentioned in
the text, there is an overarching principle of caring for the
less fortunate or vulnerable among the Israelites. However,
the question is, what does it mean to love the resident alien
as oneself? In other words, are there things that could be
done to the foreigner that would not violate that principle in
its ancient context, though such actions might seem to
contrast or contradict the same principle applied today?

Let me provide a modern example of this: let's say that, in
100 years, it becomes illegal to spank your children. If
someone were to read 100 years from now about a father

spanking his child in 2020 as a form of punishment, they would likely consider that to be immoral from their modern standards. They might ask, therefore, "How could that father *both* love his child *and* spank him? That seems contradictory." In other words, the father loving *and* spanking his child are not mutually exclusive, though they might seem to be from that future perspective. In our example, the father believes (right or wrong) that he is behaving morally when he disciplines his child by spanking him. It would be incorrect to attempt to explain away *either* the father's love for his child *or* the fact that he spanked him.

We can find similar examples of this in the Old Testament text. There is no question, for example, that fathers loved their children in the ancient world. However, we read in Proverbs 13:24, "Whoever spares the rod hates their children, but the one who loves their children is careful to discipline them." In Proverbs 22:15 we see, "Folly is bound up in the heart of a child, but the rod of discipline will drive it far away." Finally, in Proverbs 23:13, "Do not withhold discipline from a child; if you punish them with the rod, they will not die." Now, to be clear, *I am in no way advocating that we should punish our children in this way.* My only point here is that it would be incorrect for me to say, "It is immoral for someone today to spank their child. Therefore, a parent who disciplined in this way in the Bible didn't really love their child; how could they love them and do such a thing?"

There are other passages that describe similar situations. As we have seen, in Exodus 21:7 we read, "If a man sells his daughter as a servant, she is not to go free as male servants do." Wow… that sounds pretty bad to our 21st century ears. A father sold his daughter as a slave? That father must not have loved his daughter, because I love *my* daughter, and *I* would not sell her as a slave. Of course, we understand this type of behavior to be immoral today (and rightfully so), but to impose that morality on the father in Exodus 21 is to impose our understanding of morality on him. We cannot say that he did not love or care for his daughter because he sold her as a female slave, as odd as that might sound to us today.

The same would hold true for Exodus 21:20-21, where a master beats his slave with a rod as a form of discipline. While this rightfully seems horrific to us, in Proverbs 29:19-21 we read:

> "Servants cannot be corrected by mere words;
> though they understand, they will not respond.
> Do you see someone who speaks in haste?

There is more hope for a fool than for them. A
servant pampered from youth will turn out to
be insolent."
(Prov. 29:19-21)

As with a child, it was assumed and expected that a master
would beat his slave. Michael Fox notes concerning this
passage:

"The proverb gives advice for managing a
household. Since a slave is deprived of
material interests of his own, he must, it was
presumed, be beaten into submission, like a
brute animal or a fool. Slaves were apparently
felt to be of qualitatively lower order . . . Strict
treatment of slaves is advised again in
29:21."[125]

In short, it would be incorrect to conclude that a particular
behavior would have been considered immoral or oppressive
in the biblical or ancient world simply because we consider it
so today. As we have seen, although fathers loved their sons,

---

[125] Fox 2009: 843.

they were to discipline them with a rod. These two things were not mutually exclusive. This is almost certainly one aspect of reconciling this seeming contradiction.

Before we move on, however, I should briefly note that there are several different types of foreigners mentioned in the biblical text. The "resident alien" (גֵּר *ger*), who lived long term in Israel, could be circumcised and assimilated into the nation. It was the resident alien that was the subject of Leviticus 19:33-34. In Leviticus 25:44-46, however, the text speaks of the "sojourner" (תּוֹשָׁב *toshav*) that was in the land and could be made a permanent slave, along with those from the "nations" (גּוֹיִם *goyim*). This is not to say that there is a clear distinction in all cases between the *ger* and the *toshav*, but the nuanced differences between these two types of foreigners may also play a part in this discussion.

But what about Exodus 12:48? "A foreigner residing among you who wants to celebrate the Lord's Passover must have all the males in his household circumcised; then he may take part like one born in the land. No uncircumcised male may eat it." The argument here is that the "foreigner" (*ger*) is allowed to celebrate the festivals of the Lord, as long as they do as the Israelites do (in this case, circumcision). Other passages carry similar implications, such as Leviticus 24:22, "You are to have the same law for the foreigner and the native-born. I am the Lord your God."

The issues surrounding the *ger* are in no way straightforward; whole books have been dedicated to understanding both the nuanced meanings of "foreigner" (*ger*), as well as the nature of and distinctions between the various types of foreigners in the Hebrew Bible.[126] For example, in Christina van Houten's book, she devotes nearly 200 pages to the analysis of the various legal contexts in which the term *ger* appears, attempting to identify who would have been considered an alien and how the laws for the alien developed over time. What is clear, however, is that foreigners who permanently resided in the land – if they adhered to the customs and regulations set forth in the law – were afforded many of the rights of citizens. Nevertheless, as we have seen, it would be incorrect to assert that, because the *ger* could participate in and be joined to the community, that this necessarily negates the possibility of foreigners

---

[126] Van Houten 2009.

being subjected to chattel slavery. These two things are simply not mutually exclusive.

Before we move on to the next objection, I thought it might be beneficial to quote Dozeman's commentary on Exodus 12:48, which demonstrates the complexities related to issues related to the various types of foreigners:

> "Five groups are distinguished from native Israelites. Verses 43-45 address the status of the foreigner (*nokrî*), the temporary resident or client (*tôšāb*), the purchased slave (*'ebed*), the hired worker (*śākîr*); vv. 47-49 focus exclusively on the resident alien (*gēr*). The groups share two common characteristics: they lack the inalienable right to own land and they are separated from the Israelite family structure. The differences among the groups are not clear. The purchased slave can be separated most easily from among the other groups because of his slave status. Such a person can be incorporated into the ritual of the Passover on condition of circumcision. The other groups probably overlap. All designate

non-Israelites who reside for different reasons
among the Israelite people in the land of
Israel. Thus the instruction anticipates the
Israelites' future life in the land. The resident
alien may simply be a person from one of the
other categories who resides for a more
extended time among Israelites. This person is
singled out as able to participate in the
Passover upon condition of circumcision. Such
a person has equal protection under the law (v.
49). The alien assumes a special position in the
Hebrew Bible. Moses identifies himself as a
resident alien (2:22). And the Israelites are
also characterized as sojourners or resident
aliens in Yahweh's land (Lev. 25:23)."[127]

As you can see, the status of foreigners in Israel is far from a
straightforward matter, and is actually quite nuanced, both
because of the differences and similarities between them, but
also because of the development of these terms through time
and in their various legal texts.

---

[127] Dozeman 2009: 286.

What we need to keep in mind is that when the text gives clear instruction concerning a particular topic, it is unwise to attempt to rationalize that instruction away by attempting to infer general principles from other passages. Leviticus 25:44-46 says that, while the Israelites could not acquire slaves from among their brethren, they could purchase them from the foreign nations around and from among the residents dwelling among them in the land. These could be treated as inheritable property and kept for life. It would be unwise – depending on one's hermeneutical approach to the text – to cite general principles of "loving one's neighbor" in order to suggest that this passage should be reinterpreted in that light. It seems far better to understand how this type of slavery – which is clearly described in the text – would not conflict with these other passages.[128]

---

[128] This in no way suggests that there are not contradictions in the biblical texts; we have cited many such variations and developments in this book. When such contradictions are found, there are many ways to approach the differences (e.g., editorial redaction).

## Objection #2

> "Doesn't the word translated "forever" (עוֹלָם
> 'olam) in Leviticus 25:46 simply mean an
> indistinct period of time, and not "forever?"
> Terms like "forever" and "eternal" can only be
> rightfully attributed to God. Thus, 'olam in
> Leviticus 25:46 must mean simply "slaves for
> an **indefinite period of time**," and could
> really just be translated, "slaves for a **six-year
> period of time.**""

This is, in my opinion, a clear example of attempting to reinterpret a verse or passage unnecessarily to make it fit into a particular interpretive model. We see in Leviticus 25:46 ("You can bequeath them to your children as inherited property and make them slaves for life, but you must not rule over your fellow Israelites ruthlessly") that foreigners could be made to serve as slaves "for life" or "forever" (Heb. עוֹלָם 'olam – Grk. εἰς τον αἰῶνα eis ton aiona). If we begin by looking up the various meanings of 'olam, we see that it generally means "a long time, duration," which is usually nuanced to mean "for all time in the future, eternity." It is interesting to note here, however, that Koehler and Baumgartner specify "but not in the philosophical sense."[129] This concept is critical to interpreting a variety of passages in the Hebrew Bible; we cannot read all of the different meanings of a particular word back into the text.

Let me illustrate with an example. In Genesis 1:1 we read about the "heavens and the earth." Now, given the context of the passage, we could justifiably translate this "world," but only in a restricted sense. "World" can have the meaning "earth" in certain contexts, or it can have the meaning "universe," which encompasses things like space, time, and all that science has revealed to us concerning the nature of reality. However, it would be incorrect to translate Genesis 1:1, "In the beginning God created the *universe*," and then read into that word "universe" all of the nuanced understanding that we have today, concluding that the writer intended all of time, space, matter, energy, etc.

In the same way, when we approach a word like "forever" or "eternal" in the biblical texts, we want to be careful to not read too much into it. For example, one might think, "Well, only God can be eternal or exist forever, and a slave cannot

---

129 Koehler and Baumgartner 1996: #6867, s.v. עוֹלָם.

be a slave 'forever,' because they will eventually die. Therefore, the word 'forever' here must be a mistranslation. It must mean, 'a long period of time,' which allows for *any* 'long period of time.'"

There are two things that should be considered here. First, how is the word *'olam* used in the Hebrew Bible? Let's take a look at some examples. In Genesis 9:16, we see that God refers to the covenant that he makes with all living creatures after the flood as "eternal" (בְּרִית עוֹלָם *brit 'olam*). From the context we see that God vowed to never again bring a flood upon the earth, and this "eternal covenant" was established. Thus, the use of *'olam* here signifies the future without end; God simply vows to never bring a flood again in the future.

In Exodus 3:15, when God reveals himself to Moses, he states that "Yahweh" is his name "forever" (לְעוֹלָם *le'olam*), and "from generation to generation." In other words, in the future, generation after generation, they would know him as Yahweh. In Exodus 12:17, Israel is commanded to celebrate a particular feast "for the generations to come" as an "eternal ordinance" (חֻקַּת עוֹלָם *chuqqat 'olam*). Year after year, generation after generation, they were to keep this feast.

Let's look at one more example: Daniel 12:2. "Multitudes who sleep in the dust of the earth will awake: some to everlasting life (חַיֵּי עוֹלָם *chayyei 'olam*), others to shame and everlasting contempt (דְּרָאוֹן עוֹלָם *dir'on 'olam*)." Thus, when we return to passages like Leviticus 25:46 and Exodus 21:6, the slave is to serve the master *le'olam* "from that point forward," "into the future (with no end in sight)," or "for all time in the future." We should not infer, for example, that the slave would serve the master for all eternity (i.e., in the afterlife). This usage should come as no surprise to us, as we today even use the word "forever" in a variety of ways: "These pets need a 'forever home'"; "He is forever playing with his hair"; "I will love you forever."

Furthermore, if we examine the Greek words and phrases that are used to translate *'olam* in these passages, we can gain a clearer understanding of the meaning of the word. In Leviticus 25:46 and Exodus 21:6, the Septuagint (an ancient Greek translation of the Hebrew Bible) translates *le'olam* with the idiomatic phrase εἰς τον αἰῶνα (*eis ton aiona*) "to the ages." This phrase is used in the Septuagint and in the New Testament 350 times, including passages like Exodus 32:13b, "I will make your descendants as numerous as the stars in the sky and I will give your descendants all this land I promised them, and it will be their inheritance *forever.*" The phrase carries the same meaning in the New Testament, and appears in places like John 6:51a, "I am the living bread that came down from heaven. Whoever eats this bread will live *forever.*" It also appears in John 4:14, "but whoever drinks the water I will give them will *never* thirst. Indeed, the water I give them will become in them a spring of water welling up to eternal life." The Greek phrase is negated here, meaning "never (in the future)."

In short, both the Hebrew *'olam* and its Greek translation *eis ton aiona* mean "the future (with no end in sight)." When we return to Leviticus 25:46 and Exodus 21:6, the period of service of the slave is what is in view. In Leviticus 25, the foreign slave is to serve the master forever, evinced by the master's right to bequeath him to his children as inheritance, just as landed property would be handed down. In Exodus 21:6, the debt slave, in order to remain with his family, would voluntarily become a permanent slave, rather than opting for release after the required six-year period of time. Because his wife and children belonged to the master, if the man wished to remain with them, he would have to become a permanent slave.

## Objection #3

> "Doesn't Leviticus 25:47-53 and the situation
> described there show that all things were
> equal for both the Israelites and the
> foreigners?"

As we have seen, Leviticus 25 contains stipulations for the
redemption of property by the individual or by their family
members, in order that the Israelites would not become
destitute and have their land end up in the hands of only the
wealthy few in the nation. Every 50th year, the year of
jubilee, property and people were to be returned, and all
debts of Israelites were to be forgiven. However, this left
open the question of a poor Israelite who sold himself to a
sojourner who had means enough to purchase him.

In this case, the *toshav* "sojourner, tenant farmer" had
become wealthy enough to lend money to an Israelite, who
could no longer pay it back, and therefore sold himself into
debt-slavery. A relative of the Israelite was to redeem his
relative back from the foreigner.

> "If a foreigner residing among you becomes
> rich and any of your fellow Israelites become
> poor and sell themselves to the foreigner or to

a member of the foreigner's clan, they retain
the right of redemption after they have sold
themselves. One of their relatives may redeem
them: An uncle or a cousin or any blood
relative in their clan may redeem them. Or if
they prosper, they may redeem themselves.
They and their buyer are to count the time
from the year they sold themselves up to the
Year of Jubilee. The price for their release is to
be based on the rate paid to a hired worker for
that number of years. If many years remain,
they must pay for their redemption a larger
share of the price paid for them. If only a few
years remain until the Year of Jubilee, they
are to compute that and pay for their
redemption accordingly. They are to be treated
as workers hired from year to year; you must
see to it that those to whom they owe service
do not rule over them ruthlessly."
(Lev. 25:47-53)

This passage makes it clear that not all foreigners in the land
of Israel were destitute or had become slaves to the
Israelites. Indeed, some of them had wealth, and at times

greater wealth than some members of the Israelite citizenry. This neither negates the existence of foreign slaves, nor the laws concerning foreign slaves seen just a few verses earlier. It only indicates that sojourners could establish wealth in the land, which is in no way unexpected.

Objection #4

> "The position of 'slave' was highly honored in the Old Testament. Many people were referred to as a 'slave,' including Moses, David, and even the Suffering Servant in Isaiah. Certainly, you are not arguing that Moses or David were chattel slaves?"

It is absolutely true that the word "slave" in the Old Testament and in the ANE was applied to individuals of high status. For example, Moses is referred to several times as "the servant of the Lord" (Deut. 34:5; Josh. 1:1; 2 Kings 18:12). In the ANE, kings were commonly referred to as "slaves" or "servants" of the gods, or even of other kings who controlled their territory.[130] In each of these examples, the high-ranking individual is under the authority of the king or the deity, either as a form of self-effacement, or with theological nuance. In none of these cases, however, would the "slave" have the actual characteristics of a debt- or chattel-slave as we are describing here.

The contexts in which "slave" is used to refer to debt- or chattel-slaves shows that the position of a slave is in no way sought after. When we considered the laws concerning slavery in the Covenant Code of Exodus 21, we saw that a Hebrew slave was to serve only six years, to be released in the seventh. This regulation was made more beneficial in Deuteronomy 15, where the release was to be accompanied by substantial provisions by the master. When we came to Leviticus 25, however, the law required that Israelites no

---

[130] There are a multitude of examples, but see Edzard 1997: 39, E3/1.1.7.StC, ii 14-19, "(then) did Gudea, ruler of Lagaš, who is very intelligent indeed and who is a slave beloved by his mistress [a deity]." See also many examples in the Amarna Correspondence in Moran 1992. For example, pg. 221 (EA 138): "To the king, [my] lord, [the Su]n of all countries: Message of Rib-Ad[d]I, your [ser]vant. I fall beneath the feet of the king, [m]y lord, 7 times and 7 times."

longer treat their brethren as slaves, but rather hired workers. It is clear that the position of slave in this context was not a position of honor to be sought after, but one of dishonor and to be avoided, if possible.

In short, terms can carry a variety of meanings and nuances in different contexts; the use of "slave" need not carry all the implications of debt- or chattel-slavery in every situation in which it appears. While high-ranking or important individuals are referred to as "slaves" or "servants" in certain contexts, this in no way implies that all aspects of debt- or chattel-slavery were applied to that individual. We know from the biblical texts in particular that slavery was a situation to be avoided, and that the Israelites were eventually no longer allowed to make slaves of their fellow Israelites.

## Objection #5

> "If slaves were considered 'property,' then they would have had no rights and their situation would have been of no benefit to them. Slavery and rights are mutually exclusive."

There are two questions to answer here. First, were slaves considered chattel? As we have seen, there were different types of slaves in the Hebrew Bible, but primarily the text speaks of debt-slaves and chattel-slaves. Leviticus 25:44-46, for example, describes the foreign slave as one who can be kept for life and passed on as inheritance, being identified as property. Does this mean, however, that slaves – whether debt- or chattel-slaves – were given no rights under the law? It does not. We not only see slaves given rights in the Hebrew Bible, but we also see rights being accorded to slaves in the wider ancient Near East.

Beginning with the biblical texts, slaves were to have the right to rest on the Sabbath (Exod. 20:10; 23:12; Deut. 5:14) and were to be circumcised in order to participate in aspects of the cult (Exod. 12:44; Deut. 12:12, 18; Lev. 22:11). As we have discussed, the slave had the right to be free from excessive beatings and outright abuse, and could not be killed with premeditation by the master. We know that similar rights were provided to slaves in the ancient Near East as well. For example, law 117 in the laws of Hammurabi stipulates that a debt-slave had the right to release after three years of service, compared to the six years in the Hebrew Bible. Laws 170-171 give rights to the slave wife of a

174

master, providing her with freedom after the death of her master, and either the right to live in the estate, or even an equal portion of the property after his death. More generally, slaves were allowed to conduct their own cases in court concerning their freedom, calling witnesses and testifying themselves during the Ur III Period, and during the New Kingdom in Egypt, slaves could own fields and give evidence in court. These types of rights were often possessed by slaves in the ancient Near East.

Now, to be clear, I am in no way trying to soften or explain away the incredibly difficult situation in which slaves found themselves in the ancient world, whether inside or outside of Israel. My only point here is to demonstrate that, while the Hebrew Bible does likely provide some developments in the humane treatment of slaves, the life of a slave was one of turmoil and exhaustion. Dandamayev writes, "A slave's life was associated with exhausting labor, and the slave was longing for shadows like a hireling waiting for his wage."[131] In fact, J.P.M. van der Ploeg argues:

---

[131] Dandamayev 1992: 66.

"It has been said very often that slavery in
Israel, or in the Near East as a whole, should
not be put in line with classical Greek and
Roman slavery. Slaves were not too numerous
and their position was very often that of
(unfree) house servants. If they had good
masters, they were maintained by them and
were in a position very often preferable to free
but poor people. But in spite of this
consideration, slavery was an evil."[132]

A final note should be made about the idea that the master
was the only one who benefited from a master/slave
relationship. Again, a balanced approach should be
maintained with this aspect of slavery. Of course there was a
benefit to the master; the slave was his property, and the
work performed by the slave would directly benefit the
master. However, the slave received benefits as well,
including food and shelter. In Deuteronomy and Leviticus we
see that Israelite debt-slaves were to be released either with
provisions to aid in their economic re-establishment (Deut.

---

[132] Van der Ploeg 1972: 83.

15) or they were to be treated as hired workers rather than as slaves (Lev. 25). Non-Israelite slaves were not afforded these latter benefits. However, neither these rights or benefits in any way indicate that slavery is not being described in the text, and that slaves in many situations were considered property.

Objection #6

> "God told the Israelites to love and care for the foreigners. That means that they could not possibly have treated them like slaves. This was completely different from the way that foreigners were treated in the rest of the ancient world. God was doing something new in the nation of Israel."

There is no question (as we discussed above) that the Old Testament calls for the care and protection of the weak and under privileged, including the resident alien. In fact, this was a common theme in the ancient Near East. For example, in Mesopotamia, during the early part of the second millennium B.C.E., the laws of Eshnunna made provisions to protect the foreigner from unfair treatment that could easily befall him given his foreign status. In law 41, for example, we read, "If a foreigner, a *napṭaru*, or a *mudû* wishes to sell his beer, the woman innkeeper shall sell the beer for him at the current rate."[133] Concerning this, Westbrook writes, "A foreigner could acquire a protected status from the local ruler and thus become a resident alien (*ubarum*). LE 41 protects the resident alien along with other categories of outsider from economic exploitation by a taverness."[134]

Concerning the latter part of the second millennium, Slanski writes:

> "A *narû* passage reads: 'Whensoever in the future, be he Elamite, or Subarian, or Amorite, or Akkadian, officer, magistrate, who would come forward and litigate...' This passage suggests that any of those persons so identified had access to the legal system. Most *narûs* prohibit ordering a foreigner (*aḫamma*) or a stranger (*nakra*) to violate the monument . . . Sanction for violating the monument is to fall

---

[133] Roth 1997: 65.
[134] Westbrook 2003b: 377.

upon the native-born person who would take advantage of a foreigner's ignorance in order to violate the entitlement."[135]

In Ugarit, near the end of the second millennium, Rowe observes:

> "Resident aliens were members of the community . . . they did enjoy most of the rights and obligations of citizenship, such as owning land . . . Foreign visiting agents (*ubru*) and *ḫapiru*'s[(!)] also enjoyed a protected status, namely, the hospitality of the king, but were hardly subject to domestic law."[136]

To sum up, the protection of resident foreigners was a common theme in the ancient Near East, and its presence in the laws of the Hebrew Bible is certainly no surprise. This in no way negates the reality of slavery, either in the ancient Near East or in the Old Testament law.

---

[135] Slanski 2003: 497 (L. 7076).
[136] Rowe 2003: 723.

Objection #7

> "Even if there was slavery in the Old
> Testament, if a slave chose to run away, the
> law said that they could not be returned to
> their master (Deut. 23:15-16). You couldn't
> keep someone as a slave against their will."

This is another oft-mentioned and disputed passage. "If a
slave has taken refuge with you, do not hand them over to
their master. Let them live among you wherever they like
and in whatever town they choose. Do not oppress them"
(Deut. 23:15-16). The obvious question, however, is
"Concerning whom is this law written?" There are several
options. First, the runaway slave could refer to a Hebrew
debt-slave who had escaped from his Israelite master. The
language of verse 16, however, seems to indicate that this
slave did not have property to return to in the land of Israel;
he would "choose" from one of the cities that pleased him.
Were he an Israelite, he would have an allotted portion of
land to which he would return. Thus, there are problems
seeing this as an Israelite slave.

A second option is that this describes how to treat a foreign
chattel slave who had escaped from his Israelite master.

While this solves the problem of property seen above, it presents another problem. It seems odd that the law in Deuteronomy 23 would not contain a punishment for the abusive master that would have caused the slave to flee. Of course, this absence certainly does not negate the possibility that this is who is being referred to, as the law may simply not be dealing with that particular issue in the context. Thus, it is contextually possible, it would appear, that this could refer to a foreign slave who was fleeing an Israelite master.

I am of the opinion, however, that there is a third possibility that more adequately fits with the context; the text is most likely referring to a foreign slave who had escaped from slavery in a surrounding foreign nation. The idea here would be, if a foreign slave were to escape to Israel, the Israelites were not to return them to their foreign master, but were to treat them well and provide them with a place to live. It is this third option (one fleeing from a foreign land to Israel) that most scholars adhere to. See the following scholarly opinions:

Raymond Westbrook:

> "It was recognized by early commentators that
> this provision could not apply to domestic
> slavery, since it would have undermined the
> right to recover property upon which the whole
> institution depended. It makes perfect sense,
> however, when applied to the international
> sphere, where no right of recovery existed
> unless expressly authorized by treaty. The
> passage can therefore be seen as a polemic
> against such treaty provisions, and a
> prohibition on the authorities in Israel against
> ever including an extradition clause in their
> treaties with neighboring states. Mendelsohn
> suggested that it applied only to a Hebrew
> slave fleeing from a foreign master. The terms
> of the law which granted the fugitive a choice
> of dwelling in any city negate this
> interpretation. A Hebrew slave would have
> returned to his home, not picked a city to dwell
> in. By that grant of choice of dwelling and the
> injunction not to oppress him, the foreign
> fugitive was being granted the status of

resident alien without geographical limitation, which would protect him from being enslaved by an Israelite."[137]

Kenneth Kitchen:

"Slaves that fled from one country to another came under a different category. States sometimes had mutual extradition clauses in their treaties; this may explain how Shimei so easily recovered two runaway slaves of his from King Achish of Gath in Philistia (1 Ki. ii. 39, 40; . . . ). However, some states also at times decreed that if any nationals of theirs enslaved abroad returned to their homeland they would be set free and not be extradited . . . and is probably the meaning of Dt. xxiii. 15f."[138]

---

[137] Westbrook 2009b: 213-214.
[138] Kitchen 1962: 1197.

Harry Hoffner:

> "As we shall see below, in Israel slaves who
> had escaped from masters in a foreign land
> were not to be returned (Deut. 23:15-16). One
> reason for this may have been that Israel was
> not to enter into diplomatic relations with the
> surrounding pagan nations. Treaties with
> these lands would inevitably have contained
> extradition clauses."[139]

Jeffrey Tigay:

> "Virtually all commentators hold that this law
> refers to slaves who flee from foreign countries
> to Israel. 'He shall live with you among the
> settlements in your midst' (v. 17) seems to
> imply that previously the slave had been in a
> foreign land and not in Israelite territory. If
> the law referred to an Israelite slave it would
> probably have described him as 'your
> kinsman.' It would also have addressed the

---

[139] Hoffner 2008: 146.

individual householder with whom the slave
sought refuge, but the phrase 'in your midst'
and the stipulation that the fugitive may settle
anywhere in the land imply that the law is
addressed to the nation as a whole or to a
national authority."[140]

Gene Haas:

"In contrast to laws of other ancient Near
Eastern nations, slaves who flee their owners
and come to Israel are not to be returned to
their masters, nor are they to be oppressed,
but they are to be allowed to live wherever
they please (Deut. 23:15-16)."[141]

Again, I am not attempting to argue that I am correct simply
because the scholars cited above share the same
interpretation. I am merely providing the current scholarly
consensus, in line with the stated objectives of this book.

---

[140] Tigay 1996: 215.
[141] Haas 2003: 781.

Of course, there are *many* other objections that people might raise concerning the issues of slavery in the Hebrew Bible, but the questions that were answered in this chapter are raised with greater frequency, and thus deserve (in my opinion) specific attention. The details of slavery in the ancient world are sometimes difficult to identify with precision, as with any endeavor concerning historical reconstruction. What is important here, I think, is to establish the fundamental "data points" concerning slavery, and build an interpretive model that best accounts for these data points. In other words, I often see people beginning with a conclusion that they wish/believe to be true, and from there they analyze the data to reach that conclusion. Instead, we should begin by determining what the evidence can tell us about slavery in the ancient world, and from there move to models that best fit those facts.

# CONCLUSION

Perhaps the most common question that I hear concerning slavery in the ancient world is, "Did the Old Testament condone or endorse slavery?" To condone something generally implies allowing something that is known to be immoral. To endorse, however, most frequently carries the idea of publicly supporting or approving of something. One of the goals of this book was to demonstrate that the Hebrew Bible and the laws contained therein endorsed slavery; in order to demonstrate this, we not only had to determine that slavery was a reality in the Hebrew Bible, but also that the Old Testament established laws for its appropriate practice. As the following quote – and hopefully the arguments in this book – clearly demonstrate, both debt-slavery and chattel-slavery, while regulated in the legal texts, were endorsed in the Old Testament.

> "Slavery is a condition acknowledged in the
> Pentateuch in which a person is deprived of
> freedom, at least for a period of time, by being
> in subjection to a master in order that the
> master may benefit from the labor of the slave.
> Slavery may be involuntary, in which case the

187

slave is generally considered the property of the owner and, as such, may be bought and sold. In Pentateuchal legislation, involuntary permanent slavery applies only to non-Israelites. Slavery may also be voluntary for Israelites, such as when they agree to work for fellow Israelites for a limited period of time to pay off debts or to survive poverty and destitution. But, because God brought the Israelites out of slavery in Egypt to serve him alone as master, they are forbidden to bring fellow Israelites into a condition of permanent slavery, as was the case in the rest of the ancient Near East. Permanent slavery is permitted only for a Gentile in subjection to a Hebrew. The Israelites' identity as people redeemed from slavery has direct implications for the forms of slavery that existed in Israel and their treatment of their slaves, both

Gentile chattel slaves and Hebrew bondservants."[142]

In chapter one, we provided an overview of slavery in the Hebrew Bible, describing the different types of slavery that appear in the text, as well as their associated characteristics. We distinguished between debt-slaves and chattel-slaves, whether slavery was voluntary or involuntary, and the differences between regulations for Hebrew slaves and those for individuals from foreign lands. We also surveyed the general practices with respect to war plunder, and briefly described the general rights to which slaves were entitled.

In chapter two, we examined the wider ancient Near East, and how slavery appeared in that context. We began by briefly describing the nature of ancient Near Eastern law, correcting some misunderstandings that many people have concerning how the legal system functioned. We noted that, while things like law "codes" were most likely not normative, they represented a strong legal tradition that remained rather consistent throughout the ancient Near East, both geographically and diachronically. We then examined the

---

[142] Haas 2003: 778.

Conclusion

various sources for slavery at our disposal, and how it was to be practiced from the perspective of the legal tradition.

In chapter three, we provided selected commentary and exegesis on the various passages in the Hebrew Bible that deal with the issue of slavery. These included Exodus 21, Deuteronomy 15, 20, and Leviticus 25. Many significant issues were discussed, including the developments in the laws seen from the Covenant Code of Exodus 21 to Deuteronomy 15 and Leviticus 25. We examined important passages such as Exodus 21:20-21 (the beating of a slave), Deuteronomy 15 (the release of the female slave), Deuteronomy 20 (taking slaves as plunder and so-called POWs), and Leviticus 25 (foreign slaves).

Finally, in chapter four, having discussed and addressed a wide variety of the most common questions concerning slavery in the Hebrew Bible, we identified several other frequently asked questions that are pertinent to the issue of slavery, including the runaway slave of Deuteronomy 23:15-16 and the apparent contraction between the practice of slavery and the love that the Israelites were to show to foreigners in passages like Leviticus 19:33-34.

In the end, it is clear that slavery was not only condoned in the Hebrew Bible, but the legal stipulations in place demonstrate that its authors endorsed the practice. In the Anchor Bible Dictionary's entry on "slavery," concerning the purchase of slaves from neighboring nations, Dandamayev writes:

> "This source was in every possible way encouraged by biblical instructions (Lev. 25:44-46, etc.; cf. Eccls. 2:7). Such slaves were legally considered the absolute property of their owners, and their status was permanent: they were sold, passed on by way of inheritance, pawned, and branded or marked like livestock (cf. Isa. 44:5)."[143]

Slavery was not endorsed arbitrarily, as it was part of a common economic system that existed in ancient Israel, and in the wider ancient Near East long before the biblical period. Both debt-slavery and chattel-slavery were also part of the Mosaic Law, and the regulations on its practice in the text are generally on par with the other legal systems in the

---

[143] Dandamayev 1992: 66.

region, both synchronically and diachronically. In other words, generally speaking, the laws seen in the Old Testament are part of a common legal system or tradition that can be seen in the ancient Near East.

The reality of slavery in the laws of the Hebrew Bible is not only the overwhelming consensus view on slavery in the Old Testament among scholars in the field, but is not even a debated issue in scholarly circles. Slavery existed, of that there can be little doubt. The various legal texts, including those in the Hebrew Bible, make specific provisions for the practice in the hopes that it would be carried out appropriately. In some ways, to debate the endorsement of slavery in the Hebrew Bible would be akin to asking, "Does the Old Testament endorse killing people?" Of course it does. However, there were restrictions and provisions in the law that sought to ensure that people could only kill or be killed in certain circumstances (e.g., as punishment for a crime or during a time of war). The laws gave their proverbial stamp of approval on killing in these particular circumstances.

It seems to me that the question before us should not be, "Does the Old Testament endorse slavery?", but rather, "How should we understand the biblical texts and the god of the

Hebrew Bible in light of his endorsement of slavery in the Old Testament?" To be sure, many people have sought to exaggerate the nature of Old Testament slavery in an attempt to argue for a particular point of view.[144] At the same time, many others have attempted to downplay the reality of slavery in the Hebrew Bible, making it out to be nothing more than a person owning a credit card or working at a fast food restaurant. However, neither position is correct, and neither position is necessary. One can be a Christian, for example, in spite of the endorsement of slavery in the Old Testament. At the same time, one need not exaggerate the details or motives of Old Testament slavery in order to combat one's faith in the biblical text; the reality of the practice will most likely suffice.

In conclusion, it has been my goal to demonstrate as accurately as possible what the laws concerning the practice

---

[144] The prophet Amos, for example, considered the mass sale of entire populations into slavery – ostensibly for strictly monetary gain – to be abhorrent and deserving of divine retribution (Amos 1:6; 9). This, of course, does not indicate that God was against slavery, but the mass misuse of people groups.

Conclusion

of slavery were like as described in the various passages of
the Hebrew Bible, arguing that it was endorsed in the legal
system. I often say that it is not my intent to show the god of
the Old Testament to be an immoral "big meanie," or to
characterize him as a type of moral monster. Instead, my
hope is that the reader will view Old Testament slavery laws
and the legal tradition with which they accord as a product of
their cultural milieu, and that the morality that is seen in
the biblical texts can be taken, not as prescriptive laws that
must be followed throughout human history, but as
representative norms that describe practices as they existed
in the ancient world.

# Appendix A
# Source Index

## Hebrew Bible

# Appendix B

# Topic Index

# Bibliography

Achenbach, Reinhard, Albertz, Rainer & Wohrle, Jakob.

    2011   *The Foreigner and the Law: Perspectives from the Hebrew Bible and the Ancient Near East.* Beihefte zur Zeitschrift für altorientalische und biblische Rechtsgeschichte, Bd. 16. Wiesbaden: Harrassowitz Verlag.

Baker, David.

    2015   The Humanisation of Slavery in Old Testament Law. Pp. 13-20 in *The Humanisation of Slavery in the Old Testament*, ed. T. Schirrmacher. World of Theology Series 8. Eugene, OR: Wipf & Stock.

Blenkinsopp, Joseph.

    1988   *Ezra-Nehemiah.* Old Testament Library. Philadelphia, PA: Westminster Press.

Beaulieu, Paul-Alain.

    2018   *A History of Babylon 2200 BC-AD 75.* Blackwell History of the Ancient World. Hoboken, NJ: Wiley Blackwell.

Blenkinsopp, Joseph.

    1988  *Ezra-Nehemiah*. Old Testament Library.
       Louisville, KY: John Knox Press.

Bottéro, Jean.

    1992  *Mesopotamia: Writing, Reasoning, and the*
       *Gods.* Chicago, IL: University of Chicago
       Press.

Chirichigno, Gregory.

    1993  *Debt-Slavery in Israel and the Ancient Near*
       *East.* Sheffield: JSOT Press.

Christensen, Duane.

    2001  *Deuteronomy 1:1-21:9, Second Edition.* Word
       Biblical Commentary. Nashville, TN: Thomas
       Nelson.

Collins, John.

    2018  *Introduction to the Hebrew Bible*, 3rd Edition.
       Minneapolis, MN: Fortress.

Colson, F. H.

    1998  *Philo, Volume VII.* Trans. F.H. Colson. Loeb
       Classical Library 320. Cambridge, MA:
       Harvard University Press.

Cook, Stephen.

    2018   *Ezekiel 38-48: A New Translation with Introduction and Commentary.* Anchor Yale Bible Commentaries. New Haven, CT: Yale University Press.

Copan, Paul.

    2011   *Is God a Moral Monster? Making Sense of the Old Testament God.* Grand Rapids, MI: Baker Books.

Culbertson, Laura.

    2011   Slaves and Households in the Near East. Pp. 1-17 in *Slaves and Households in the Near East*, ed. L. Culbertson. Oriental Institute Seminars 7. Chicago, IL: University of Chicago.

Dandamayev, Muhammad.

    1984   *Slavery in Babylonia: From Nabopolassar to Alexander the Great (626-331 B C).* DeKalb, IL: Northern Illinois University Press.

    1992   Slavery. Pp. 58-65 in *The Anchor Bible Dictionary, Vol. 6*, ed. D. Freedman. New York, NY: Doubleday.

Dozeman, Thomas.

2009   *Exodus*. Eerdmans Critical Commentary.
Grand Rapids, MI: Eerdmans.

Durham, John.

2015   *Exodus*. Word Biblical Commentary. Grand
Rapids, MI: Zondervan.

Edzard, Dietz Otto.

1997   *Gudea and His Dynasty*. The Royal
Inscriptions of Mesopotamia: Early Periods.
Volume 3/1. Toronto: University of Toronto
Press.

Falk, Ze'ev.

2001   *Hebrew Law in Biblical Times*. Winona Lake,
IN: Eisenbrauns.

Fox, Michael.

2009   *Proverbs 10-31*. Anchor Yale Bible
Commentaries. New Haven, CT: Yale
University Press.

Frymer-Kenski, Tikva.

2003   Anatolia and the Levant: Israel. Pp. 975-1046

in *A History of Ancient Near Eastern Law*, ed.
R. Westbrook. 2 vols. Leiden: Brill.

Garroway, Kristine.

2014    *Children in the Ancient Near Eastern
Household.* Explorations in Ancient Near
Eastern Civilizations. Winona Lake, IN:
Eisenbrauns.

Gerstenberger, Erhard.

1996        *Leviticus.* Old Testament Library. Louisville,
KY: Westminster John Knox.

Grabbe, Lester.

1987    Fundamentalism and Scholarship: The Case of
Daniel. Pp. 133-152 in *Scripture: Meaning and
Method. Essays Presented to Anthony Tyrrell
Hanson for His Seventieth Birthday*, ed. B.
Thompson. Yorkshire, England: Hull
University Press.

Greengus, Samuel.

1997    The Selling of Slaves: Laws Missing from the
Hebrew Bible? *ZABR* 3: 1-11.

Gurtner, Daniel.

    2013   Exodus: A Commentary on the Greek Text of
            Codex Vaticanus. Leiden: Brill.

Haas, Gene.

2003        Slave, Slavery. Pp. 778-783 in *The Dictionary
            of the Old Testament: Pentateuch*, ed. D. Baker
            and T. Alexander. Downers Grove, IL:
            InterVarsity Press.

Haase, Richard.

    2003   Anatolia and the Levant: The Hittite
            Kingdom. Pp. 619-656 in *A History of Ancient
            Near Eastern Law*, ed. R. Westbrook. 2 vols.
            Leiden: Brill.

Hamilton, Victor.

    1990   *The Book of Genesis 1-17*. New International
            Commentary on the Old Testament. Grand
            Rapids, MI: Eerdmans.

Harrison, R. K.

    1980   *Leviticus: An Introduction and Commentary*.
            Tyndale Old Testament Commentaries.
            Downers Grove, IL: InterVarsity Press.

Hoffner, Harry.

    2008   Slavery and Slave Laws in Ancient Hatti and Israel. Pp. 130-155 in *Israel: Ancient Kingdom or Late Invention?*, ed. D. Block. Nashville, TN: B&H Publishing.

Van Houten, Christiana.

    2009   *The Alien in Israelite Law: A Study of the Changing Legal Status of Strangers in Ancient Israel.* Sheffield: JSOT Press.

Jackson, Bernard.

    2006   *Wisdom-Laws: A Study of the Mishpatim of Exodus 21:1-22:16.* Oxford: Oxford University Press.

Jasnow, Richard.

    2003a Egypt: Old Kingdom and First Intermediate Period. Pp. 93-140 in *A History of Ancient Near Eastern Law*, ed. R. Westbrook. 2 vols. Leiden: Brill.

    2003b Egypt: New Kingdom. Pp. 289-359 in *A History of Ancient Near Eastern Law*, ed. R. Westbrook. 2 vols. Leiden: Brill.

    2003c Egypt: Third Intermediate Period. Pp. 777-818

in *A History of Ancient Near Eastern Law*, ed.
R. Westbrook. 2 vols. Leiden: Brill.

Joosten, Jan.

1996 *People and Land in the Holiness Code: An
Exegetical Study of the Ideational Framework
of the Law in Leviticus 17-26.* Leiden: Brill.

Kitchen, Kenneth.

1962 Slave, Slavery. Pp. 1195-1199 in *The New
Bible Dictionary*, ed. J. D. Douglas. Grand
Rapids, MI: Eerdmans.

Kline, Meredith.

1958 The Ha-BI-ru, Kin or Foe of Israel?
*Westminster Theological Journal* 20: 46-70.

Koehler, Ludwig and Baumgartner, Walter.

1996 *The Hebrew and Aramaic Lexicon of the Old
Testament*, Volume 3. Leiden: Brill.

Lafont, Bertrand and Westbrook, Raymond.

2003 Mesopotamia: Neo-Sumerian Period (Ur III).
Pp. 183-226 in *A History of Ancient Near
Eastern Law*, ed. R. Westbrook. 2 vols. Leiden:
Brill.

Lafont, Sophie.

2003 Mesopotamia: Middle Assyrian Period. Pp.
521-563 in *A History of Ancient Near Eastern
Law*, ed. R. Westbrook. 2 vols. Leiden: Brill.

Levine, Baruch A.

1989 *Leviticus*. The JPS Torah Commentary. New
York, NY: Jewish Publication Society.

Levinson, Bernard.

2005 The Birth of the Lemma: The Restrictive
Interpretation of the Covenant Code's
Manumission Law by the Holiness Code (Lev
25:44-46). *JBL* 124: 617-639.

2006 The "Effected Object" in Contractual Legal
Language: The Semantics of "If You Purchase
a Hebrew Slave" (Exod. XXI 2). *VT* 56: 485-
504.

Longman III, Tremper.

1997 *The Book of Ecclesiastes*. New International
Commentary on the Old Testament. Grand
Rapids, MI: Eerdmans.

Magdalene, Rachel F. and Wunsch, Cornelia.

> 2011 Slavery Between Judah and Babylon: The
> Exilic Experience. Pp. 113-134 in *Slaves and
> Households in the Near East*, ed. L.
> Culbertson. Oriental Institute Seminars 7.
> Chicago, IL: University of Chicago.

Magdalene, Rachel F., Wunsch, Cornelia, and Wells, Bruce.

> 2019 *Fault, Responsibility, and Administrative Law
> in Late Babylonian Legal Texts.
> Mesopotamian Civilizations.* University Park,
> PA: Eisenbrauns.

Mayshar, Joram.

> 2014 Who Was the Toshav? *Journal of Biblical
> Literature* 133: 225-246.

Mendelsohn, Isaac.

> 1978 *Slavery in the Ancient Near East: A
> Comparative Study of Slavery in Babylonia,
> Assyria, Syria, and Palestine, from the Middle
> of the Third Millennium to the End of the
> First Millennium.* Reprint Edition. Westport,
> CT: Greenwood Press.

Meyers, Carol.

> 2005 *Exodus.* New Cambridge Bible Commentary. New York, NY: Cambridge University Press.

Milgrom, Jacob.

> 2000 *Leviticus 17-22: A New Translation with Introduction and Commentary.* Anchor Bible Yale Commentaries. New Haven, CT: Yale University Press.

> 2001 *Leviticus 23-27: A New Translation with Introduction and Commentary.* Anchor Bible Yale Commentaries. New Haven, CT: Yale University Press.

Moran, William.

> 1992 *The Amarna Letters.* Baltimore, MD: Johns Hopkins University Press.

Morrow, William.

> 2017 *An Introduction to Biblical Law.* Grand Rapids, MI: Ecrdmans.

Muraoka, Takamitsu.

> 2009 *A Greek-English Lexicon of the Septuagint.* Walpole, MA: Peeters.

Nelson, Richard.

    2002  *Deuteronomy*. Old Testament Library.
          Louisville, KY: Westminster John Knox.

Oelsner, Joachim, Wells, Bruce, and Wunsch, Cornelia.

    2003  Mesopotamia: Neo-Babylonian Period. Pp.
          911-974 in *A History of Ancient Near Eastern
          Law*, ed. R. Westbrook. 2 vols. Leiden: Brill.

Olley, John.

    2009  *Ezekiel: A Commentary Based on Iezekiēl in
          Codex Vaticanus*. Leiden: Brill.

Ownes, J. Edward.

    2011  *Leviticus*. New Collegeville Bible
          Commentary. Collegeville, MD: Liturgical
          Press.

Porten, Bezalel.

    2003  Egypt: Elephantine. Pp. 863-881 in *A History
          of Ancient Near Eastern Law*, ed. R.
          Westbrook. 2 vols. Leiden: Brill.

Phillips, Anthony.

    1984  The Laws of Slavery: Exodus 21.2-11. *JSOT*
          30: 51-66.

Propp, William.

    1999   *Exodus 1-18: A New Translation with Introduction and Commentary.* Anchor Bible Yale Commentaries. New Haven, CT: Yale University Press.

    2006   *Exodus 19-40: A New Translation with Introduction and Commentary.* Anchor Bible Yale Commentaries. New Haven, CT: Yale University Press.

Radner, Karen.

    2003   Mesopotamia: Neo-Assyrian Period. Pp. 883-910 in *A History of Ancient Near Eastern Law*, ed. R. Westbrook. 2 vols. Leiden: Brill.

Roth, Martha.

    1997   *Law Collections from Mesopotamia and Asia Minor.* Atlanta, GA: Scholars Press.

Rowe, Ignacio.

    2003   Anatolia and the Levant: Ugarit. Pp. 719-735 in *A History of Ancient Near Eastern Law*, ed. R. Westbrook. 2 vols. Leiden: Brill.

Sarna, Nahum.

1991   *The JPS Torah Commentary: Exodus.* Philadelphia, PA: Jewish Publication Society.

Schirrmacher, Thomas.

2015   *The Humanisation of Slavery in the Old Testament,* ed. T. Schirrmacher. World of Theology Series 8. Eugene, OR: Wipf & Stock.

Seow, Choon-Leong.

2008   *Ecclesiastes: A New Translation with Introduction and Commentary.* Anchor Yale Bible Commentaries. New Haven, CT: Yale University Press.

2013   *Job 1-21: Interpretation and Commentary.* Illuminations. Grand Rapids, MI: Eerdmans.

Sklar, Jay.

2014   *Leviticus.* Tyndale Old Testament Commentaries. Downers Grove, IL: Inter Varsity Press.

Slanski, Kathryn.

2003   Mesopotamia: Middle Babylonian Period. Pp.

485-520 in *A History of Ancient Near Eastern Law*, ed. R. Westbrook. 2 vols. Leiden: Brill.

Thompson, J. A.

1995 *The Book of Jeremiah*. New International Commentary on the Old Testament. Grand Rapids, MI: Eerdmans.

Tigay, Jeffrey.

1996 *The JPS Torah Commentary: Deuteronomy*. Philadelphia, PA: Jewish Publication Society.

Tsai, Daisy Yulin.

2014 *Human Rights in Deuteronomy: With Special Focus on Slave Laws*. Germany: De Gruyter.

Van der Ploeg, J. P. M.

1972 Slavery in the Old Testament. Pp. 72-87 in *Congress Volume Uppsala 1971*, ed. P. A. H. Boer. VT Supplements 22. Leiden: Brill.

Veenhof, Klaas.

2003 Mesopotamia: Old Assyrian Period. Pp. 431-483 in *A History of Ancient Near Eastern Law*, ed. R. Westbrook. 2 vols. Leiden: Brill.

Westbrook, Raymond.

2003a The Character of Ancient Near Eastern Law.
Pp. 1-90 in *A History of Ancient Near Eastern
Law*, ed. R. Westbrook. 2 vols. Leiden: Brill.

2003b Mesopotamia: Old Babylonian Period. Pp. 361-
430 in *A History of Ancient Near Eastern Law*,
ed. R. Westbrook. 2 vols. Leiden: Brill.

2003c Anatolia and the Levant: Emar and Vicinity.
Pp. 657-691 in *A History of Ancient Near
Eastern Law*, ed. R. Westbrook. 2 vols. Leiden:
Brill.

2009a Cuneiform Law Codes and the Origins of
Legislation. Pp. 73-95 in *Law from the Tigris
to the Tiber: The Writings of Raymond
Westbrook*, eds. R. Magdalene and B. Wells.
Winona Lake, IN: Eisenbrauns.

2009b Slave and Master in Ancient Near Eastern
Law. Pp. 161-216 in *Law from the Tigris to the
Tiber: The Writings of Raymond Westbrook*,
eds. R. Magdalene and B. Wells. Winona Lake,
IN: Eisenbrauns.

Westbrook, Raymond and Wells, Bruce.

    2009  *Everyday Law in Biblical Israel.* Louisville, KY: Westminster John Knox.

Wilcke, Claus.

    1996  Neue Rechtsurkunden der Altsumerischen Zeit. *Zeitschrift für Assyriologie und Vorderasiatische Archäologie* 86: 1-67.

    2003  Mesopotamia: Early Dynastic and Sargonic Periods. Pp. 141-181 in *A History of Ancient Near Eastern Law*, ed. R. Westbrook. 2 vols. Leiden: Brill.

    2007  *Early Ancient Near Eastern Law: A History of Beginnings. The Early Dynastic and Sargonic Periods.* Winona Lake, IN: Eisenbrauns.

Woods, Edward.

    2011  *Deuteronomy.* Tyndale Old Testament Commentaries. Downers Grove, IL: InterVarsity Press.

Wright, David.

    2009  *Inventing God's Law: How the Covenant Code of the Bible Used and Revised the Laws of Hammurabi.* Oxford University Press.

Zaccagnini, Carlo.

    2003   Mesopotamia: Nuzi. Pp. 565-617 in *A History of Ancient Near Eastern Law*, ed. R. Westbrook. 2 vols. Leiden: Brill.

Made in the USA
Columbia, SC
30 November 2022

72357389R00140